JAPANESE PAPER CRAFT

AYA NAGAOKA

JAPANESE PAPER CRAFT

A GUIDE TO MAKING YOUR OWN BOOKS, NOTEPADS, AND KEEPSAKES

AYA NAGAOKA

Hardie Grant

NORTH AMERICA

CONTENTS

3. ORGANIZING

4. ARCHIVING

Stationery is all around us through life...

Crayons held when we are children, first learning the world around us. Brand-new pencils and notebooks for primary school. Flashcards for university exams. Folders and sticky notes needed for work. A box of supplies that inspires us to pursue our hobbies. A photo album that brings back family memories...

Many kinds of stationery, each with their own purpose, discretely accompany us at the edges of our lives. And because they are always there, they should be things that we truly like. If you've ever seen a product on the shelf and thought, "if only it had this," now you can make your wish come true. You can choose colors you like, make it in a shape or form that suits your needs, and add your own features.

In this book, I offer 30 stationery projects, divided into groups of ten by purpose: writing, organizing, and archiving. Some are simple and can be completed in a few hours, while others may take a few days, but the fundamental steps are universally familiar: cutting, folding, and gluing.

Stationery made from paper particularly lends itself to be handcrafted. And the more you make your own, the more fun the making becomes; the more you use your stationery, the deeper your affection for it will become. The act of crafting can calm the mind and soul. So to make your everyday just a little more creative, why don't you give Japanese papercraft a try?

Aya Nagaoka

I. TECHNIQUES

USING THIS BOOK

This book is organized thematically with projects of varying difficulties. There is a rough progression but you do not need to work from cover to cover; you may choose projects from any section and, once you are comfortable with making stationery, please adjust the designs to your personal needs. If you are new to papercraft, however, I recommend you first familiarize yourself with the bookbinding terms and basic techniques (cutting, folding, gluing, wrapping, sewing, and others) in this section, before progressing onto the projects.

For each project, you will find a list of all the materials used along with the size of the project (all sizes are given in millimeters). Further breakdowns of material sizes are given in the figures and instructions. For more information on paper types and thicknesses, see pages 14–15, "Materials." Then follow the figures: diagrams of the various components of each project, including the locations for the folds and holes and the method of stitching. In this section, and throughout, the following symbols are used:

Mountain fold (the outside of the fold):   ----------
Valley fold (the inside of the fold):   — — — —
Glue area: ▒▒▒▒
Direction of the paper grain: ⟺
Units: mm

Under method you will find the step-by-step instructions for making the project. For instructions on the fundamental techniques (cutting, folding, gluing, wrapping, sewing, and others), please refer to pages 16–21. For more information on the tools required, see pages 12–13, "Tools." Most projects use PVA and starch glue or starch paste. You can make starch glue at home (see below) and you can find starch paste from specialist stores. A note on adhesives:

· PVA glue: Use a kind made for paper and bookbinding.
· Starch glue: A 1:1:1 mixture of PVA glue, starch paste, and water.
· Starch paste: Used when working with washi.
(See pages 12–13, "Tools," for more information.)

Conversion charts from metric to imperial are located throughout the book. Conversions of the materials required for the various projects can be found on the corresponding section openers. A conversion chart, located on the back cover flap, shows conversions for any additional measurements associated with the projects' methods.

BOOKBINDING TERMS

Paperback Books

Books with a thin,
non-paperboard cover.

Hardcover Books

Books with a cover material wrapped around paperboard.

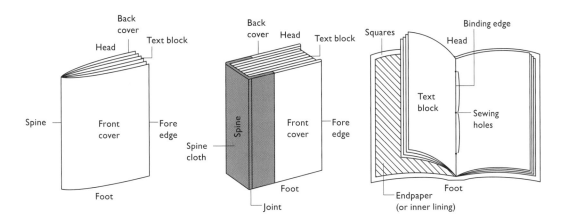

Head/foot: The top-facing side is called the head, and the bottom-facing side is the foot.

Spine: The bound side of the book.

Spine cloth: Cloth that connects the front and back covers.

Joint: The groove running along the spine on the front and back covers.

Fore edge: The side opposite the spine.

Binding edge: The inner (bound) edge of the text block.

Text block: The pages that constitute the inside of a book; the primary content. The "text block thickness" indicates the width visible between the front and back covers when closed.

Sewing holes: Holes made for passing thread through when binding pages.

Squares: The margins where a book's front and back covers extend beyond the endpapers and text block. The squares along the head, fore edge, and foot are generally preferred to be of equal size.

Endpaper/inner lining: The paper glued to the inner side of the front and back covers. In this book, I use the term "endpaper" when the object contains pages, and the term "inner lining" for objects that don't.

Envelopes

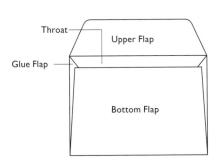

Boxes

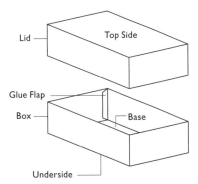

TOOLS

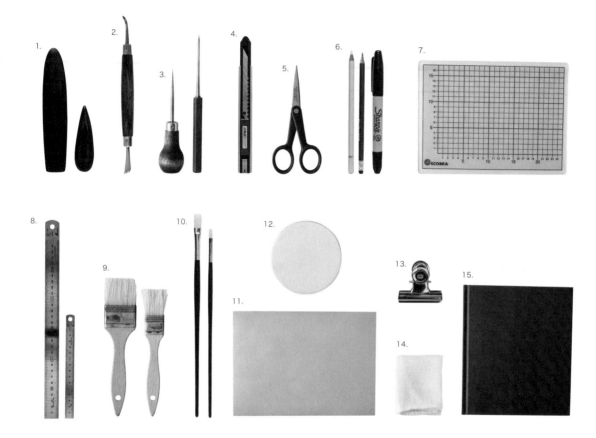

1. Paper folder: For folding paper or wrapping over paperboard.

2. Scorer: For adding creases to paper.

3. Awl: For punching holes for stitching. When driving with a wooden mallet, use an awl whose metal extends through the grip (right).

4. Craft knife: The go-to knife for cutting straight lines.

5. Scissors: For rounding corners.

6. Writing Implements: For marking locations of holes, guidelines on the underside of paper, and more. Depending on the color and qualities of the material, I may use a white pencil, pen, or marker.

7. Cutting mat: Used when cutting with a craft knife and also as a general work surface. The grid lines come in handy.

8. Metal ruler: Metal rulers with the zero on the tail end.

9. Paint brushes: Wide brushes for applying adhesive. Choose a width suitable for the surface area.

10. Artist's paint brushes: Small brushes for applying adhesive to smaller areas.

11. Kraft paper: For protecting paper from damage that might result from direct contact with tools.

12. Weight: For applying pressure. Can also hold materials in place during stitching and gluing.

13. Hinge clips: For temporarily fastening materials together. Two clips are more stable than one.

14. Cloth: For pressing across the surface of your materials when gluing.

15. Work surface: A thick, hardcover book or a piece of wood can serve as a work surface when stitching or applying glue. They also can be used as weights.

16. PVA glue: Some formulations are specially made for paper and bookbinding. Choose glue that is fast drying and strong. Use in places that need a strong hold.

17. Starch glue: A 1:1:1 mixture of PVA glue, starch paste, and water.

18. Starch paste: Used when working with Japanese (washi) or handmade paper. Note that starch pastes are slow to dry.

19. Glue stick: For gluing small pieces.

20. Multi-purpose glue: For gluing materials other than paper.

21. Double-sided tape: Used when glues or pastes would be impracticable.

22. Masking tape: For making temporary joins.

23. Needle-nose pliers: Use one in each hand to open jump rings.

24. Tweezers: For delicate operations.

25. Rubber mat: A heavy-duty rubber mat used as a work surface when hammering with a wooden mallet.

26. Wooden mallet: For punching round holes with an awl or hollow punch, and for setting rivets and eyelets.

27. Hollow punch: Also called a hammer-driven punch. Strike with a wooden mallet to punch holes in your material. Select an appropriate diameter for your work.

28. Hole punch: Use when making a hole near the edge of the paper.

29. Corner punch: For rounding corners.

30. Double-cap rivet tools: Choose a rivet setter and anvil that fit the size of the rivets being used.

31. Eyelet tools: For common diameters, the easiest method is to set with a portable hand press (right). If the hand press cannot reach, use an eyelet setter and anvil that matches the size of the eyelet being used.

32. Hemp thread: For stitching, hardy hemp thread is ideal.

33. Needle: Used when stitching. To avoid damaging the paper, use a thick, fairly blunted, specialty bookbinding needle.

34. Beeswax: Before sewing, wax your thread to prevent fraying. (Further explained on page 20.)

MATERIALS

Paper Grain

During the manufacture of paper, most paper fiber becomes aligned in a single direction, called the grain. The grain direction of your paper can affect your final product in various ways, such as being hard to open or easy to break. For the purposes of this book, when I recommend a particular grain direction, it is indicated by a double-headed, outlined arrow within the project's figure section: .   ⟺

Locating the Grain Direction when Purchasing Paper

Long Grain   Short Grain

When purchasing paper, the grain may be indicated as "long grain" or "LG" or "short grain" or "SG"; by an underline beneath the dimension corresponding with the grain's direction; or by the second number in the paper's dimension. In Japan, long grain paper is labeled T-Grain (T-Me) and short grain paper is labeled Y-Grain (Y-Me).

Determining the Grain Direction by Hand

 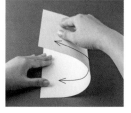

You can also determine the grain direction of a given sheet of paper by its pliability. Paper will fold more easily parallel to the grain (left) and more resistant perpendicular to the grain (right).

Paper Thickness

Paper comes in a variety of thicknesses. One joy of making your own stationery is tailoring the thickness of the paper to your specific liking. Just beware that for certain uses, such as binding a book, paper that is too thick or too thin will make the work more difficult. In this book, the paper thicknesses are noted in the materials lists.

Paper Weight Guide

Approx. 65 gsm	A little lighter than typical printer paper. Used from newsprint to note-books.
Approx. 80 gsm	Typical printer paper, paper used inside magazines, fliers.
Approx. 115 gsm	Typical promotional posters.
Approx. 150 gsm	Magazine covers, CD jackets.
Approx. 210 gsm	Typical postcards, business cards.
Approx. 230 gsm	Thicker postcards, passbook covers.
Approx. 350 gsm	Packaging for cosmetics or liquor bottles.

Paper weight is measured in GSM (grams per square meter). A higher number corresponds to heavier and thicker paper.

Composite Paper

In several of my projects, I glue two different types of paper together to make my work material, which I call "composite paper." This method can be used to adjust paper thickness and to explore the effects of difference combinations of paper.

I. Spread a uniform layer of starch glue well across the underside of one sheet of paper. For paper of different thicknesses, apply the glue to the thicker paper.

2. Place the glued side onto a second, larger sheet of paper. Smooth well and apply firm pressure on both sides. Place weight on top and let rest overnight.

3. Once the paper is completely dry, cut to your desired size.

Caution: Gluing paper can easily result in warping. For best results, work quickly and don't skimp on smoothing and pressing.

Common Paper Types

These are the most common types of paper and bookbinding cloth I use in the projects in this book. I primarily use materials with a matte texture for their warmth and relative ease of use. Specialty paper can be purchased from art supply stores, and the paperboard and bookbinding cloth from stores that specialize in bookbinding materials.

NT Rasha
I use this paper in the majority of these projects. NT Rasha paper is easy to use and comes in a wealth of thicknesses and colors.

1. Jean Felt Has a distinctive felt-like texture.
2. Satogami Evokes a sense of pastoral nostalgia.
3. Mermaid Its texture is like gentle waves.
4. GA File Thick paper with a natural feel.

Patterned Paper
Use patterned paper (such as wrapping paper) for endpapers or inner linings. I use this in my composite paper in several projects.

Notebook Paper
When selecting paper for the inside of a notebook or memo pad, choose it with a writing feel you enjoy—whether that's lined paper, graph paper, kraft paper, manilla drawing paper, or anything else.

Washi
Strongly textured, traditional handmade paper. Use starch paste when adhering. Tearing it can create an interesting, expressive edge.

Translucent Paper
Examples include tracing paper and glassine. Take care when working with them as they are easily damaged.

Paperboard
Thick paper used for the covers and spine of hardback books. In these project, I use 1–2 mm-tick paperboard.

Bookbinding Cloth
Cloth lined with thin paper. Though primarily used in bookbinding, it is also used in making cartonnage and stationery.

CUTTING

Cutting Paper and Bookbinding Cloth

Hold your craft knife like a pencil. The material you are cutting should lie face up, oriented so that the cutting line is vertical in front of you. Use your non-dominant hand to firmly hold the ruler in place.

Cutting Paperboard

Make an initial shallow cut to score the material, then cut along the same line several times. Take care not to apply too much pressure in an attempt to cut all the way through on the first attempt, and ensure the knife's blade is not cutting at an angle.

Wet Tearing Washi

1. Position a metal ruler along the desired cut line and trace along the ruler's edge with a wetted brush.

2. While still holding the ruler in place, pull the paper from the side to tear.

Making Holes

When using a hollow punch:

Place the punch directly on the material where you wish to make a hole, then strike the punch with a wooden mallet.

When using a hole punch:

To better locate the hole, remove the bottom cover from the hole punch and operate it upside down.

Rounding Corners

When using scissors:

For best results, draw a guideline with a pencil before cutting.

When using a corner punch:

A corner punch can be used on right-angle corners to easily create uniformly rounded corners.

Cutting Slits

For narrow slits (1mm):

Make a hole at each end of the slit, draw a line connecting the center of each hole and use a craft knife to cut along both sides of the line.

For wider slits:

Make a hole at each end of the slit and use a craft knife to cut from the outside edges of one hole to the other.

FOLDING

Folding With a Paper Folder

For paper weights up to around 115 gsm

1. Gently bend the paper over. Use your non-dominant hand to align the corners.

2. While holding the corners in place, take your paper folder with your dominant hand and place it on the fold at your nearest side and at an angle.

3. Slide the paper folder at an angle toward the far edge of the fold.

Folding With a Score Line

For paper weights greater than 150 gsm or when working in small areas such as glue flaps.

1. Place a metal ruler along what will be the inner side of the fold (the valley) and run your scorer along the ruler's edge.

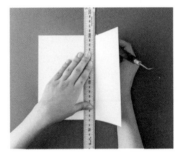

2. Holding the ruler in place, place your scorer beneath the paper and slide to lift the paper from below.

3. Remove the ruler and press with your paper folder to make a crisp fold.

Brushing With Water

For creating a better fold in a stack of folded pages, as with a text block.

1. Stack the folded pages together and hold them firmly so that the folded edge remains aligned.

2. Brush water onto the folded edge. Move the brush up and down so that the head and foot sides remain dry.

3. Leave a weight on top for a while, and you will have a clean fold.

GLUING

(For types of glue, consult pages 12–14 on Tools and Materials)

Spreading Glue

When applying adhesive to a flat surface, such as a book cover, bookbinding cloth, or endpaper.

1. Using a wide brush, spread the adhesive outward in a radial pattern, using your non-dominant hand to hold the paper in place.

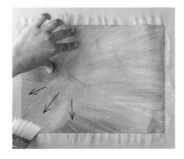

2. Reposition your non-dominant hand and fill in the remaining space.

3. Make sure there aren't any empty gaps or excess pools of glue and then remove any unwanted debris with tweezers.

Pressing

After spreading the glue and adhering your materials, immediately smooth the entire surface by applying pressure with a cloth.

When gluing flat materials:

Through a sheet of kraft paper, smooth both sides of the glued materials with a cloth.

When gluing across a groove:

Through a sheet of kraft paper, use a paper folder to apply pressure also in the grooves.

When gluing a box:

Insert the kraft paper into the box and reach in with your cloth to apply pressure. The same technique applies within pockets.

Gluing Flaps

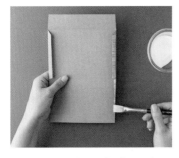

Spread glue onto the glue flap. For good results, also apply glue to edge of the matching surface where the flap will be glued.

Gluing a Fixed Width

Brush toward the outside

Place kraft paper over the material so that the glue will only be applied where you want it.

Placing Weights

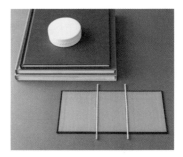

Place the glued material between kraft paper or paperboard and place books or weights on top. When the material includes joints or grooves, place a skewer or rolled-up paper in the depressions.

WRAPPING

Wrapping Over Paperboard

Wrapping bookbinding cloth or paper around paperboard to make book covers and more.

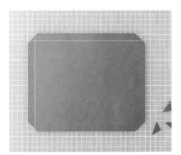

1. Trace lines on the underside of the paper 15 mm from the head and left edges. If there is a joint or groove in the paper, mark that as well. Cut a 20 mm triangle from each corner of the paper.

2. Brush starch glue evenly across the underside of the paper. Take care as some types of paper have a greater tendency to warp.

3. Place the paperboard along the traced lines. The starch glue won't set immediately; take advantage of this time to position the paperboard just right.

4. Fold the paper over, beginning with the head and foot edges. Using your non-dominant hand, pull the paper while folding and gluing with your dominant hand to eliminate any slack from the fold.

5. Apply firm pressure with a paper folder along the glued material. If there is a joint or a groove, press with the edge of the paper folder to form a tight bond.

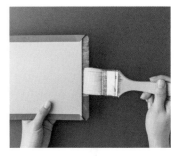

6. If the starch glue has begun to dry on the left and right flaps, reapply a small amount.

7. For crisp corners, use the paper folder to fold any excess material inside.

8. Fold and glue the left and right flaps in the same manner as the head and foot, and then flatten with the paper folder.

9. Turn the paper over, place kraft paper on top, and smooth with a cloth and firm pressure. If you are also gluing an endpaper or inner lining, do so now. Place a weight on top of your material and let rest overnight.

SEWING

Creating Sewing Holes

When making a hole in a folded text block:

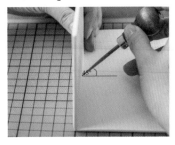

Open the text block to a 90 degree angle, hold an awl at a 45 degree angle, and punch all the way through to the outermost page.

When making a straight up-and-down hole:

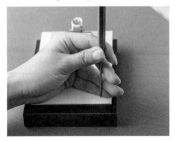

When making holes in something like a notepad, support an awl with your hand and keep it vertical as you strike with a wooden mallet until the hole is all the way through.

Preparing the Needle and Thread

Waxing thread:

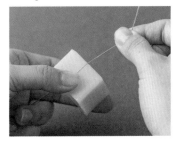

Draw hemp thread along the beeswax two to three times. The wax will protect against fraying and loose stiches.

Tying the thread to the needle (bookbinder's knot):

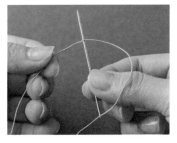

1. Once you have threaded the needle, unspool about 50 mm of thread, then pass the needle through the strands of the thread.

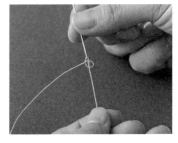

2. Pull on the longer thread to secure the thread to the needle.

Additional Tips

Positioning:

Sewing will be easier near the edge of a raised surface such as a desk. Put the spine of the book in front of you at the edge of the raised surface and place a weight on top of the book to keep it in place.

Pulling the thread:

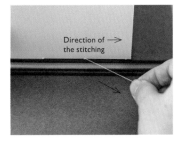

Each time you come out through the material, pull the thread toward the direction of your progress to keep the stitching tight.

Using a paper folder:

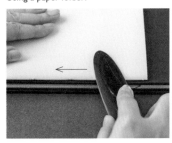

Once you are done sewing, use the flat side of a paper folder to remove swelling in the paper along the spine.

OTHER

Setting Eyelets

When using an eyelet setter:

When using portable hand press:

1. Make a hole matching the size of the tube of the eyelet, then insert the eyelet.

2. Place the eyelet setter on top and hammer with a wooden mallet.

Punch the hole with the press, then insert the eyelet and set it with the press.

Setting Rivets

1. Punch a hole matching the rivet's post and insert the post into the material.

2. Place the cap on top of the post and the rivet setter on top of the cap, then hammer with a wooden mallet.

Setting Jump Rings

1. Grasp the ring with two pairs of needle-nose pliers and twist the ends apart.

2. Pass the ring through the material and bend the ends back together. Take care not to damage the paper with the pliers.

Inserting Elastic Cords

1. Punch a hole in the material and pass the elastic cord through. Then insert an eyelet or rivet into the same hole.

2. Set the eyelet or rivet to fix the elastic cord in place. Leaving a tail of 2–3 mm, cut the rest.

Preventing Fraying

Using the side of a brush, apply a small amount of wood glue to the cut edge of the elastic cord or ribbon. Wait for the glue to dry before using.

(Note: Do a dry fit of the eyelet or rivet and confirm the elastic cord's orientation and fit before continuing.)

CONVERSION CHART

01 Notebook

Cover	180 × 368mm	7.08 x 14.48in
Text block	170 × 170mm	6.69 x 6.69in
	60 × 170mm	2.36 x 6.69in
	104 × 170mm	4.09 x 6.69in
Elastic	170mm	6.69in

02 Fastened Letter

Envelope	320 × 260mm	12.60 x 10.24in
Lining	295 × 260mm	11.61x 10.24in
Letter	100 × 200mm	3.94 x 7.87in
Header	100 × 60mm	3.94 x 2.36in

03 Memo Pad

Cover	85 × 240mm	3.35 x 9.45in
Bookbinding cloth	50 × 95mm	1.97 x 3.74in
Text block	105 × 74mm [A7]	4.13 x 2.91in

04 Rough Pad

Cover	14 × 182mm	.55 x 7.16in
Base	257 × 182mm [B5]	10.12 x 7.16in
Text block	200–257 × 182mm	7.87-12.1 2 x 7.16in

05 Postcard Kit

Outer paper	255 × 331mm	10.03 x 13.03in
Glassine paper	60 × 145mm	2.36 x 5.70in
Leather strap	50 × 10mm	1.97 x .39in
Elastic cord	120mm	4.72in

06 Tiny Book

Bookbinding cloth	52 × 76mm	2.04 x 2.99in
Cover backing	36 × 60mm	1.42 x 2.36in
Text block	40 × 460mm	1.57 x 18.11in

07 Flip Book

Cover	40 × 120mm	1.57 x 4.72in
Text block	40 × 120mm	1.57 x 4.72in

08 Sketchbook

Bookbinding cloth	260 × 212mm	10.24 x 8.34in
Paperboard	230 × 182mm	9.05 x 7.16in
Lining	224 × 176mm	8.81 x 6.92in
Text block	230 × 182mm	9.05 x 7.16in
Elastic cord	500mm	19.68in

09 Washi Notebook

Washi paper	200 × 320mm	7.87 x 12.60in
	155 × 240mm	6.10 x 9.45in
	104 × 160mm	4.09 x 6.30in

10 Clipboard

Front side	270 × 350mm	10.63 x 13.78in
Paperboard	240 × 320mm	9.45 x 12.60in
Underside	234 × 314mm	9.21 x 12.36in
Elastic cord	80mm	3.15in
	30mm	1.18in

2. WRITING

NOTEBOOK

A three-in-one notebook

Three separate books, each bound with hemp thread, collected into one notebook. This notebook is easily portable while allowing for division of purposes (for example: meeting notes, to-do lists and personal notes). By customizing the layout, including the number of inside books and their proportional sizes, you can make your own original notebook.

materials

- Cover: 1 sheet 180 × 368 mm paper (approx. 230 gsm)
  (The example uses two kinds of paper glued together.)
- Text block: 10–20 sheets each 170 × 170 mm; 60 × 170 mm; and
  104 × 170 mm paper (notebook paper, kraft paper, etc.)
- Hemp thread: 3 × combined height of inner books
- 1 piece approx. 170 mm elastic cord

size

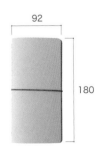

92

180

figures

Fig. A (Cover)

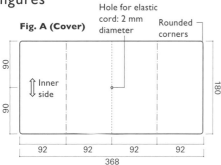

Hole for elastic cord: 2 mm diameter

Rounded corners

Inner side

90

90

92 92 92 92

368

180

Fig. B (Text Block)

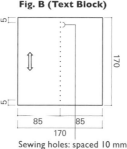

5

170

5

85 85

170

Sewing holes: spaced 10 mm apart for 17 in total

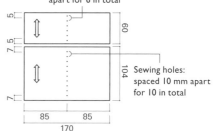

Sewing holes: spaced 10 mm apart for 6 in total

5

7.5

60

104

7

85 85

170

Sewing holes: spaced 10 mm apart for 10 in total

Fig. C (Stitching)

When sewing through an odd number of holes, start with the centermost; with even numbers, start with the one closest to the center. For example, with five holes, as shown here, bind 1 and 9 with a square knot around 5.

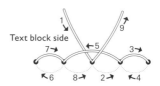

Text block side

1
9
7→ ←5 3→
←6 8→ 2→ ←4

method

1. Score and crease the cover paper to create the fold lines. Use a corner punch to round the corners, and punch the hole for the elastic cord (Fig. A).

2. Fold the text block paper in half with a paper folder (page 17). Open the pages and stack them.

3. Mark the locations for the sewing holes along the crease of the innermost page (Fig. B).

4. Place the text block onto the cover so that the squares are even, then hold the text block and cover open at a 90 degree angle. Using an awl, punch the sewing holes at a 45 degree angle.

5. Sew the book into the cover (Fig. B; page 20). Repeat steps 2–5 with the remaining inner books.

6. Tie the elastic cord into a loop, then pass the cord through the cover's central hole from the outside. The knot from the loop will keep the cord in place.

FASTENED LETTER

A letter held in place with a prong fastener

An envelope and letter combined into one with a prong fastener. The pages of the letter are read by flipping through them like a notepad. For a more memorable experience, I make the exterior plain and use a bright, colorful wrapping paper as the liner to create a more visual impact upon opening.

materials

· Envelope: I sheet 320 × 260 mm paper (approx. 230 gsm) ⓐ
· Inner lining: I sheet 295 × 260 mm paper (wrapping paper, etc.) ⓑ
· Letter: 5–10 sheets 100 × 200 mm paper ⓒ
· Header: I sheet 100 × 60 mm paper ⓓ
· I set prong fasteners

size

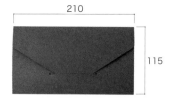

210

115

figures

Fig. A (Envelope)

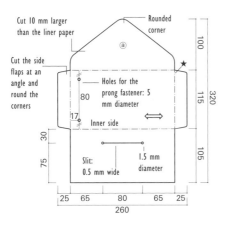

Cut 10 mm larger than the liner paper

Cut the side flaps at an angle and round the corners

Rounded corner

ⓐ

Holes for the prong fastener: 5 mm diameter

Inner side

80

17

30

75

100

320

115

105

Slit: 0.5 mm wide

1.5 mm diameter

25 65 80 65 25

260

Fig. B (Inner Lining)

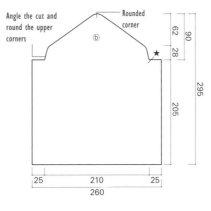

Angle the cut and round the upper corners

Rounded corner

ⓑ

62

90

28

295

205

25 210 25

260

Fig. C (Header)

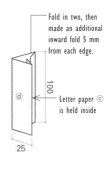

Fold in two, then made an additional inward fold 5 mm from each edge.

ⓓ

Letter paper ⓒ is held inside

100

25

method

1. Score and crease the fold lines of the envelope paper ⓐ (Fig. A).

2. Cut the liner paper ⓑ to size (Fig. B). Use scissors to round the corners of the upper flap.

3. Apply starch glue to the underside of the liner, then align the starred locations (Fig. A and B) and paste together. Smooth well across the surface, then place weight on top and leave overnight.

4. Trim (Fig. A), then use scissors to round the corners of the flaps.

5. Add a slit for the flap to pass through (page 16), then punch holes for the prong fastener (Fig. A).

6. Place the letter paper ⓒ into the folded header ⓓ (Fig. C), then use an 80 mm center-to-center two-hole punch (or a hole punch or hollow punch) to create the holes for the prong fastener. Insert the fastener.

#03

MEMO PAD

A reusable memo pad

A memo pad with a retro match-case look. I use bookbinding cloth to reinforce the portion that may wear through repeated opening and closing. The pages are held in place with brass fasteners rather than thread or glue, which allows the memo pads to be refilled and used again. A4 paper, cut into eighths, makes for a perfect fit.

materials

· Cover:
   1 sheet 85 × 240 mm paper (approx. 230 gsm)
   (The example uses two kinds of paper glued together.)
   1 piece 50 × 95 mm bookbinding cloth
· Text block: approx. 30 sheets 105 × 74 mm (A7) paper (printing paper, etc.)
· 2 brass fasteners

size

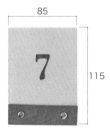

figures

Fig. A (Cover)

Bookbinding cloth: Fix 45 mm from the edge on the outer side, with 5 mm of the cloth folding over the end.

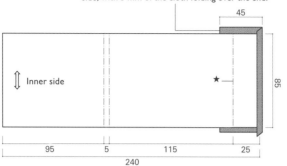

45

Inner side

★

85

95   5   115   25

240

Fig. B (Fastening)

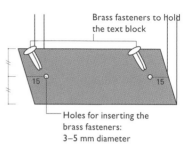

Brass fasteners to hold the text block

15   15

Holes for inserting the brass fasteners: 3–5 mm diameter

method

1. Apply starch glue to the underside of the bookbinding cloth and paste to the cover paper (Fig. A). Smooth with firm pressure, place weight on top and leave until the glue is dry.

2. Trim the bookbinding cloth flush to the cover, then score the cover paper along the fold lines (Fig. A).

3. Add a stamp of your liking to the center of what will become the front cover.

4. After having folded the starred line (Fig. A), punch the holes for the brass fasteners (Fig. B).

5. Place the text block paper inside the cover and mark the fastener holes on the top page. Punch in the holes, then use as a template for punching the other pages, a few at a time.

6. Place the text block into the cover and affix in place with the brass fasteners (Fig. B).

#04

ROUGH PAD

A notepad made from unmatched paper

Bind together leftover paper from your various notebooks into a new pad. Only five stitches peek out through the front to make the appearance as clean as possible. I purposefully choose papers of differing lengths to feature their differing colors and lines.

materials

- Cover edge: 1 sheet 14 × 182 mm paperboard (1 mm thick)
- Base: 1 sheet 257 × 182 mm (B5) paperboard (1 mm thick)
- Text block: approx. 40 sheets 200–257 × 182 mm (max B5) paper (notebook paper, etc.)
- Hemp thread: 3 × width of text block

size

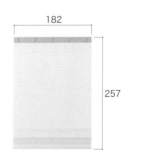

182

257

figures

**Fig. A
(Cover Edge
Paperboard)**

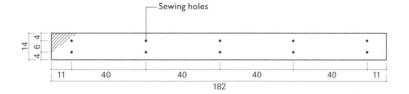

Sewing holes

14 · 4 · 6 · 4

| 11 | 40 | 40 | 40 | 40 | 11 |

182

**Fig. B
(Stitching)**

Front side

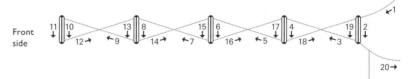

Tie the beginning and end of the thread near a sewing hole with a square knot.

---

method

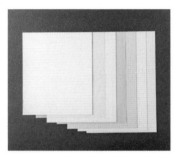

1. Arrange the text block papers portrait from shortest to longest.

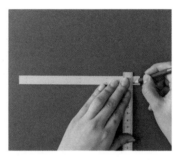

2. Mark the sewing holes on the cover edge paperboard (Fig. A).

3. Place the pad in order, starting with the base, then the text block, and then the cover edge paperboard. Neatly align the head and hold in place with hinge clips.

4. Punch the sewing holes straight down through the marks. Move the hinge clips as needed to punch every hole.

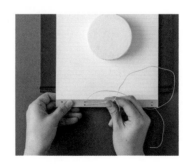

5. Sew the book (Fig. B; page 20).

6. End the stitch with a square knot and cut away excess thread. Apply a little PVA glue to the tip of an awl and push the knot into the hole.

POSTCARD KIT

A handy postcard kit for your travels

Sometimes when I'm traveling, I'll decide to mail a postcard, but then find myself without a pen or unable to get stamps, so I give up. That's why I made a portable kit containing postcards, stamps, and a pen all in a single pack that's small enough to easily fit into a bag.

materials

- · Case: 1 sheet 255 × 331 mm paper (approx. 350 gsm)
  (The example uses two kinds of paper glued together.)
- · Stamp pouch: 1 sheet 60 × 145 mm glassine paper
- · Pen holder: 50-mm long × 10-mm wide leather strap
  (adjust to fit your pen)
- · 2 × approx. 120 mm flat elastic cords
- · 5-mm diameter double-cap rivet
- · 2 brass fasteners
- · 4 × 4-mm (inside diameter) eyelets

size

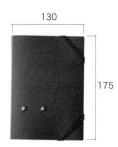

130

175

figures

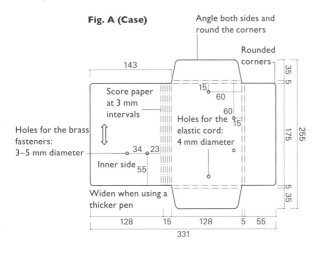

Fig. A (Case)

Angle both sides and round the corners

Rounded corners

143

Score paper at 3 mm intervals

Holes for the brass fasteners: 3–5 mm diameter

Inner side

Widen when using a thicker pen

15 / 60 / 60 / 15

Holes for the elastic cord: 4 mm diameter

34 / 23 / 55

35 / 5 / 175 / 255 / 5 / 35

128 / 15 / 128 / 5 / 55

331

Fig. B (Pen Holder)

Bend the leather strap into a circle and glue together with PVA glue. Place onto the case and punch the hole for the double-cap rivet through both the paper and the strap, then insert and set the rivet.

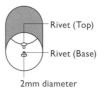

Rivet (Top)

Rivet (Base)

2mm diameter

Fig. C (Stamp Holder)

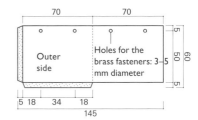

70 / 70

Outer side

Holes for the brass fasteners: 3–5 mm diameter

5 / 50 / 5 / 60

5 18 / 34 / 18

145

method

1. Score and crease the fold lines on the case (Fig. A).

2. Cut the excess material from the case (Fig. A). Use scissors to round the corners.

3. Affix the leather band with a double-cap rivet to make the pen holder (Fig. B), adjusting the location to fit your pen.

4. Cut the glassine paper to size. Apply glue to the glue flaps and fold into a pouch (Fig. C).

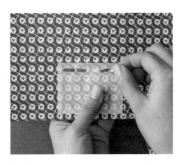

5. Place the stamp pouch onto its location on the case. Punch the brass fastener holes through both the pouch and the case, then affix the pouch with the brass fasteners.

6. Punch holes in the case for the elastic cords. Being careful not to twist them, insert the bands and affix with eyelets (page 21).

#06

TINY BOOK

A small, book-shaped notebook

Though miniature in size, this is a proper cloth-bound, hardcover book. Once you make one, you'll want to make more to line up next to each other. I came up with this design to make effective use of my scraps of bookbinding cloth. The construction is simple: an accordion-folded text block glued inside a cover. You can even write a message inside and give it alongside a gift.

materials

· Cover: 1 piece 52 × 76 mm bookbinding cloth
· Cover backing: 1 sheet 36 × 60 mm paper (approx. 230 gsm)
· Text block: 1 sheet 40 × 460 mm paper (approx. 115 gsm –
  enough for a total thickness of 4 mm when accordion folded)

size

4

36

28

figures

Fig. A (Text Block)

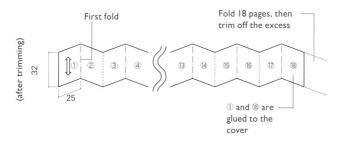

First fold

Fold 18 pages, then trim off the excess

(after trimming)

32

25

① ② ③ ④ ⑬ ⑭ ⑮ ⑯ ⑰ ⑱

① and ⑱ are glued to the cover

Fig. B (Cover)

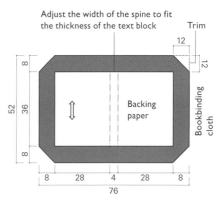

Adjust the width of the spine to fit the thickness of the text block

Trim

12

12

Bookbinding cloth

Backing paper

52   36   8   8

8   28   4   28   8

76

method

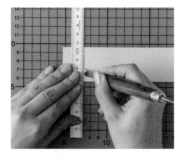

1. Score and crease the first fold in the text block (Fig. A).

2. Fold the text block accordion style, prioritizing matching the alignment of the spine and fore edge (ignore deviation along the head and foot sides).

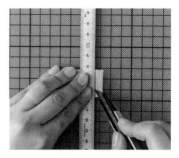

3. Trim the head and foot sides to 32 mm high.

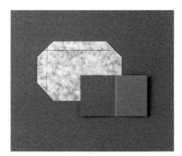

4. Trace guidelines 8 mm from the head and left edges on the underside of the bookbinding cloth, then trim the corners. Score the cover's backing paper (Fig. B).

5. Apply starch glue to the underside of the bookbinding cloth and wrap around the backing paper (page 19). When the glue is partially dry, crease along the score lines on the backing paper.

6. Apply starch glue to the reverse sides of pages ① and ⑱ of the text block and glue onto the cover, spacing the squares evenly. Smooth well across the surface, then place weight on top and leave overnight.

FLIP BOOK

An elastic-bound flip book

A flip book is usually used for viewing hand-drawn, animated pictures. The exceedingly simple elastic cord construction allows you to easily add and remove pages. The long and narrow size also neatly fits into a pocket for use as a pocket notebook.

materials

· Cover: 2 sheets 40 × 120 mm paper (approx. 115 gsm)
· Text block: several sheets 40 × 120 mm paper (enough for a
   total thickness of 5–10 mm)
· 1 elastic cord

size

120

40

figure

Figure (Cover, Text Block)

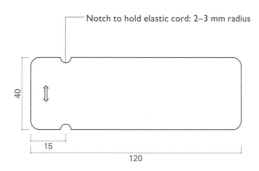

Notch to hold elastic cord: 2–3 mm radius

40

15

120

method

1. Using the hole punch upside down to better judge the placement, punch notches into the cover and text block (Fig.): Do one page first, then use as a template for punching the other pages, a few at a time.

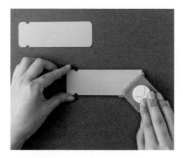

2. Use a corner punch to round all the corners.

3. Stack all the pages together with the covers on the top and bottom, then hold in place with the elastic cord in the notches.

SKETCHBOOK

A ring-bound sketchbook

This sketchbook is bound with jump rings, a versatile metal connector frequently used in jewelry and charms. The text block can consist of a mixture of several kinds of paper, including drawing paper, graph paper, kraft paper, and tracing paper. I add an elastic cord to the cover to keep the sketchbook from opening while being carried.

materials

- Cover:
    2 pieces 260 × 212 mm bookbinding cloth
    2 sheets 230 × 182 mm paperboard (1 mm thick)
- Endpaper: 2 sheets 224 × 176 mm paper (such as wrapping paper, etc.)
- Text block: several sheets 230 × 182 mm paper (drawing paper, graph paper, kraft paper, tracing paper, etc. – enough for a total thickness of 4–5 mm)
- 1 piece approx. 500 mm elastic cord
- 5 × 15 mm (inside diameter) jump rings
- 10 × 4 mm (inside diameter) eyelets

size

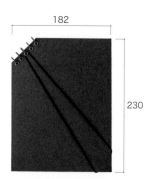

182

230

figures

Fig. A (Text Block)

The distance between the center of the holes and the edge of the paper should be smaller than half the diameter of the rings.

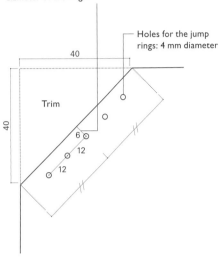

Holes for the jump rings: 4 mm diameter

40

40

Trim

6

12

12

Fig. B (Covers)

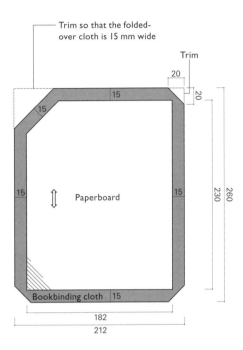

Trim so that the folded-over cloth is 15 mm wide

Trim

20

20

15

15

15

Paperboard

15

15

260

230

Bookbinding cloth 15

182

212

---

method

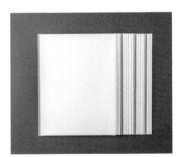

1. Arrange the various kinds of text block paper in a random order.

2. Place the stack between two pieces of paperboard and hold in place with masking tape.

3. Trim a triangle with 40 mm sides from the hinge corner (Fig. A). Once you are finished, remove the paperboards.

4. Punch holes in one page of the text block for the jump rings (Fig. A). Use as a template for punching the other pages, a few at a time.

5. For the covers: On the underside of the bookbinding cloths, trace guidelines 15 mm from the head and longer side edges, then trim the corners. The shortened corner will be mirrored between the front and back covers.

6. Apply starch glue to the underside of the bookbinding cloths and wrap around the paperboards (page 19). Wrap the shortened corner last.

(Trim the endpaper so that the square of the shortened corner is even with the other squares.)

7. Apply starch glue to the underside of the endpapers and evenly glue to the covers. Smooth well across the surface, then place weight on top and leave overnight.

8. Transfer the hole locations from the text block to the covers, then punch the holes for the jump rings.

9. Set eyelets into the holes, but in the front cover's center hole, insert the elastic cord before setting the eyelet (page 21).

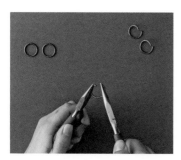

10. Grasp the jump rings with two pairs of needle-nose pliers and twist their ends apart.

11. Arrange the sketchbook's components in order (front cover, text block, back cover) and hold in place with hinge clips, then insert a jump ring into the first hole.

12. Use your needle-nose pliers to bend the jump ring back into its closed position. Repeat with the remaining jump rings.

WASHI NOTEBOOK

A handsewn notebook made from traditional Japanese paper

To fully enjoy the washi's unique texture, I purposefully avoid using a cover and fray the edges. It is bound with a French link stitch, which I love for its simplicity—all you need is a needle and thread.

materials

· Text block:
  12 sheets 200 × 320 mm washi paper (large);
  or 20 sheets 155 × 240 mm washi paper (medium);
  or 32 sheets 104 × 160 mm washi paper (small)
· Hemp thread: (number of signatures + 1) × height of text block
  from head to foot

(You will also need two pieces of spare paperboard when applying the glue to
the spine.)

size

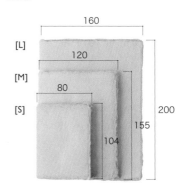

figures

Fig. A (Signatures)

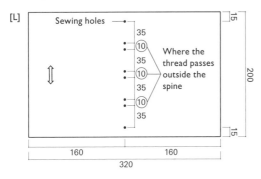

Fold the pages of the text block in half, then stack together.

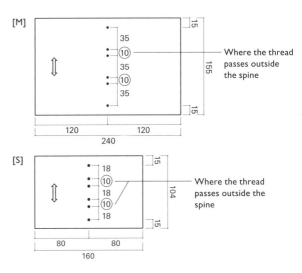

[M]

35
(10)
35
(10)
35

15

155

15

120 · 120
240

Where the thread passes outside the spine

Fig. B (Text Block)

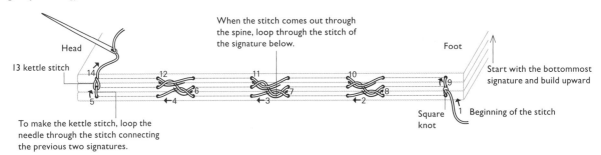

[L]

Sewing holes

35
(10)
35
(10)
35
(10)
35

15

200

15

160 · 160
320

Where the thread passes outside the spine

[S]

18
(10)
18
(10)
18

15

104

15

80 · 80
160

Where the thread passes outside the spine

Fig. C (Stitching)

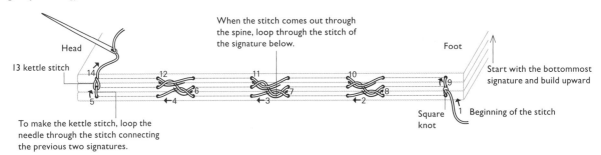

When the stitch comes out through the spine, loop through the stitch of the signature below.

Head

Foot

13 kettle stitch

14

12 11 10

6 7 8

5

4 3 2

9

1

Start with the bottommost signature and build upward

Square knot

Beginning of the stitch

To make the kettle stitch, loop the needle through the stitch connecting the previous two signatures.

---

method

1. Wet tear the text block washi to create frayed edges (page 16).

2. Fold the washi in half with a paper folder (page 17) and place in stacks of four. Each set of four is called one signature. Make as many signatures as you require (Fig. A).

3. Mark the locations for the sewing holes along the crease of the innermost page of each signature (Fig. B).

4. Open the signature to a 90 degree angle. Using an awl and the marked locations, punch the sewing holes at a 45 degree angle.

5. Leaving roughly 100 mm of the start of the thread, sew the signature with a straight stitch (Fig. C; page 20). Enter through the hole closest to the foot of the first signature and proceed to the head of that signature.

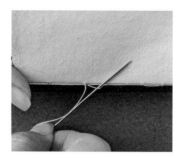

6. Stack the second signature on top of the first, then stitch the second signature in the opposite direction, from head to foot. Where your thread comes out from the spine, loop through the stitch of the signature below.

7. Once you reach the end of the second signature, tie a square knot with the beginning of the thread. Trim the thread, leaving a 3 mm tail.

8. Place the next signature on top of the previous two, and continue as before. When you reach the end of this signature, pass your needle between the previous two signatures.

9. Pass your needle through the loop to form a kettle stitch. As you continue adding signatures, make a kettle stitch at each end.

10. Once you've reached the end of your final signature, make the kettle stitch as before, followed by an additional kettle stitch between the final two signatures.

11. Trim the thread and flatten the spine with a paper folder.

(To keep the outsides of your book clean, place the book between two pieces of paperboard when applying the glue.)

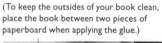

12. Apply PVA glue to the spine. Spread evenly with a paper folder, pressing the glue into the gaps between each signature. Place weight on top and leave overnight.

#10

CLIPBOARD

A clipboard with holders for writing utensils

A clipboard is a handy tool for holding and writing on documents during meetings or while standing, but I thought a clipboard could be even more handy if only it had a place to hold my writing utensils. And so I made one with easy-to-use elastic cord pen holders.

materials

- Front side: 1 sheet 270 × 350 mm paper (approx. 115 gsm)
- Board: 1 sheet 240 × 320 mm paperboard (2 mm thick)
- Underside: 1 sheet 234 × 314 mm paper (approx. 115 gsm)
- 3 pieces elastic cord:
   2 approx. 80 mm long;
   1 approx. 30 mm long
- 6 × 5-mm diameter single-cap rivets
- 4 × 2.5-mm (inside diameter) metal book corner protectors
- 1 hinge clip

size

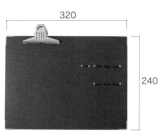

320

240

figures

Fig. A (Clipboard)

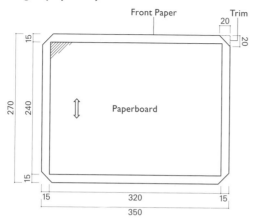

Front Paper
Trim
20
20
15
270
240
15
15
Paperboard
15
320
15
350

Fig. B (Pen Holders)

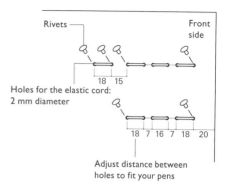

Rivets
Front side
18 15
Holes for the elastic cord:
2 mm diameter
18 7 16 7 18 20
Adjust distance between holes to fit your pens

method

1. Trim the corners of the paper for the front side of the clipboard. Apply starch glue to the reverse side of the paper and wrap around the paperboard (Fig. A; page 19).

2. Punch the holes for the elastic cords (Fig. B).

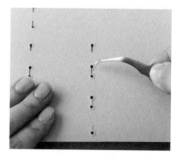

3. To make grooves for the elastic cord to run along the underside: Use a craft knife to make a shallow cut along each side of an approx. 1-mm-wide groove, then remove the inner material with tweezers.

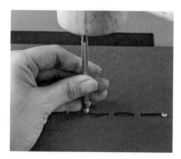

4. Pass the elastic cord through the holes and affix with a rivet at each end. For best results, fit your pens and adjust the elastic cord as needed before affixing with the rivets.

5. Apply starch glue to the paper for the underside of the clipboard and glue into place, keeping the squares even. Smooth well across the surface, then place weight on top and leave overnight.

6. Trim the corners of the clipboard slightly to fit the corner protectors. Apply a small amount of PVA glue to both the protectors and the corners and then affix the protectors.

CONVERSION CHART

11 Pen Tray

	260 × 120mm	10.24 x 4.72in
	230 × 90mm	9.05 x 3.54in
	200 × 60mm	7.87 x 2.36in

12 Sticky Note Folder

Folder	150 × 312mm	5.90 x 12.28in
Elastic cord	120mm	4.72in

13 Card Organizer

Case	141 × 268mm	5.55 x 10.55in
Paperboard	111 × 85mm	4.37 x 3.35in
Spine	111 × 60mm	4.37 x 2.36in
Inner lining	105 × 234mm	4.13 x 9.21in
Pockets	300 × 235mm	1.81 x 9.25in
Edges	15 × 300mm	.59 x 11.81in
Partitions	62 × 115mm	2.44 x 4.52in
Ribbon	180mm	7.08in

14 Booklet Box

Box	185 × 425mm	7.28 x 16.73in

05 Postcard Kit

Cover	276 × 140mm	10.87 x 5.51in
Spine	276 × 60mm	10.87 x 2.36in
Paperboard	246 × 138mm	9.68 x 5.43in
Lining	240 × 132mm	9.45 x 5.19in
Spine lining	255 × 331mm	255 × 331in
Pockets	270 × 260mm	10.63 x 10.24in
Elastic cord	290mm	11.42in

16 Document Envelope

Bookbinding cloth	40 × 285mm	1.57 x 11.22in
Buttons	15mm	.59in
Ribbon	220mm	8.66in

17 Document Folder

Cover	350 x 227mm	13.78 x 8.94in
Spine	350 x 60mm	13.78 x 2.36in
Paperboard	320 x 230mm	12.60 x 9.05in
Inner lining	314 x 220mm	12.36 x 8.66in
Spine inner lining	314 x 50mm	12.36 x 1.97in
Pockets	185 x 240mm	7.28 x 9.45in
	155 x 241mm	6.10 x 9.49in
Pockets	8 x 70mm	1.31 x 275in
Elastic cord	170mm	6.69in

18 Masking Tape Box

Drawer	120 x 350mm	4.72 x 13.78in
Outer case	178 × 191mm	7.00 x 7.52in
Base	117 × 187mm	4.60 x 7.36in
Leather strap	40 × 6mm	1.57 x .24in

19 Book Slipcase

Case	[book's height + 60mm] x [book's width x 2] + book's thickness + 100m	[book's height + 2.36in] x [book's width x 2] + book's thickness + 3.94in
Leather strap	40 x 3mm	1.56 x .2in

20 Storage Box

Base	306 × 346mm	12.04 x 13.62in
	306 x 276mm	12.04 x 10.87in
	152 × 172mm	5.98 x 6.77in
Lid	300 × 340mm	11.81 x 13.38in
	300 × 270mm	11.81 x 10.63in
	150 × 170mm	5. 90 x 6.69in

3. ORGANIZING

PEN TRAY

Nesting pen trays

Whether you are writing, crafting, or working, it feels good when the tools you need are organized and within reach. Quick to make and requiring little material, these pen trays will make your desk a pleasant space. And, because they are nesting, they can be neatly stored away when not in use.

materials

· Trays (all approx. 350 gsm):
   1 sheet 260 × 120 mm paper (large);
   1 sheet 230 × 90 mm paper (medium);
   1 sheet 200 × 60 mm paper (small)
· 12 × 4 mm (inside diameter) eyelets

size

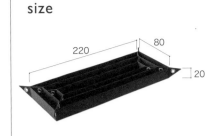

figure

Figure (Trays)

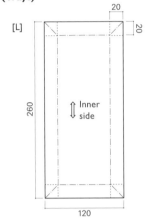

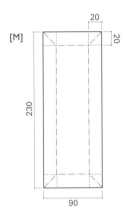

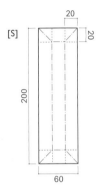

method

1. Score and crease the fold lines of each piece of paper for the trays (Fig).

2. Fold the corners together into triangles.

3. Set an eyelet at each corner triangle.

STICKY NOTE FOLDER

A folder for sticky notes, labels, and paperclips

Sticky notes end up scattered about in pencil cases, paperclips vanish, and memo pads can be hard to find right when you need them. I made this folder to remove those stresses from the day. Customize to the size of the sticky notes, paperclips, and other supplies that you frequently use.

materials

· Folder: 1 sheet 150 × 312 mm paper (approx. 350 gsm)
   (The example uses two kinds of paper glued together.)
· Approx. 120 mm elastic cord
· 3.5-mm diameter double-cap rivet

size

63

150

figure

Figure (Folder)

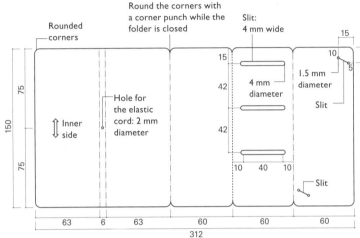

Rounded corners

Round the corners with a corner punch while the folder is closed

Slit: 4 mm wide

Inner side

Hole for the elastic cord: 2 mm diameter

15

42

4 mm diameter

42

10   40   10

15

10

1.5 mm diameter

Slit

5

Slit

150

75

75

63   6   63   60   60   60

312

Adjust the positions of the slits to match the size of the items (paperclips, memo paper, etc.) that you will be storing inside.

method

1. Score and crease the fold lines on the paper for the folder. Round the corners with a corner punch (Fig.).

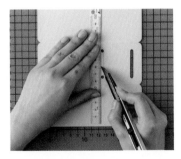

2. Add slits to hold your paper clips, memo paper, or other items (Fig.; page 16).

3. Punch the hole for the elastic cord, then insert the band and fix in place with a rivet (page 21).

CARD ORGANIZER

A pocketed organizer for business cards

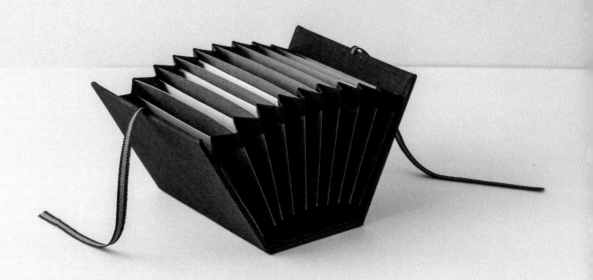

This organizer stores business cards in accordion-style pockets and sits neatly on a desktop to be fanned open when needed. Cards can be sorted into groups by each pocket and used with or without an index. Aside from business cards, this case could provide convenient storage for loyalty cards or the like.

materials

- Case:
  1 piece 141 × 268 mm bookbinding cloth ⓐ
  2 sheets 111 × 85 mm paperboard (2 mm thick) ⓑ
- Spine: 1 sheet 111 × 60 mm paperboard (2 mm thick) ⓒ
- Inner lining: 1 piece 105 × 234 mm bookbinding cloth ⓓ
- Pockets: 1 sheet 300 × 235 mm paper (approx. 115 gsm) ⓔ
- Edges: 2 pieces 15 × 300 mm bookbinding cloth ⓕ
- Partitions: 10 sheets 62 × 115 mm paper (approx. 230 gsm) ⓖ
- 2 pieces approx. 180mm ribbon

size

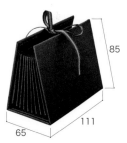

85

111

65

figures

Fig. A (Pockets)

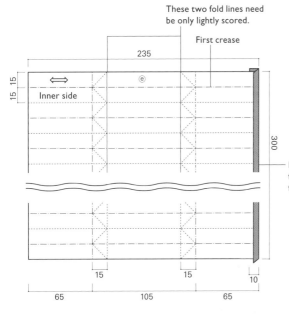

These two fold lines need be only lightly scored.

First crease

235

15 15
15

Inner side

ⓔ

300

15   15   10

65   105   65

Bookbinding cloth ⓕ: Affix 10 mm from the edge on the outer side, then fold over 5 mm into the inner side

Fig. B (Partitions)

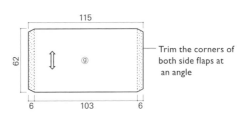

115

62

ⓖ

Trim the corners of both side flaps at an angle

6   103   6

Fig. C (Case)

Form grooves for the joints

Trim

20

20

15

141   111

15

Case paperboard ⓑ

Spine paperboard ⓒ

Case paperboard ⓑ

Bookbinding cloth ⓐ

15   85   4   60   4   85   15

268

---

method

1. Score and fold the first of the accordion folds on the paper for the pockets ⓔ (Fig. A). Continue scoring and folding the rest of the accordion folds as you go.

2. Once you reach the other end, spread the paper open again and score the vertical and diagonal folds (Fig. A).

3. Apply starch glue to the underside of the bookbinding cloth for the edges ⓕ and glue to each edge of the paper (Fig. A). Smooth firmly across the surface, then place weight on top and let rest for a time.

(Trim the top outside edges of the accordion fold at an angle.)

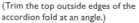

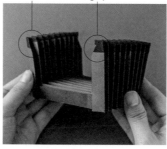

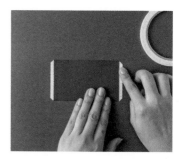

4. Starting with only one side, fold the paper along the score lines. Fold in the corners to make a right angle at the joint. Continue until one side has been folded.

5. Unfold the paper, then repeat the process, this time folding both sides up at the same time.

6. Score and crease the fold lines on the paper for the partitions ⓖ and place double-sided tape on the side flaps (Fig. B).

7. One by one, stick the partitions into the pocket folds.

8. Fix partitions to the ends of the accordion fold with PVA glue.

9. On the underside of the bookbinding cloth for the case ⓐ, trace guidelines 15 mm from the head and left edges and the guidelines for the joint grooves. Trim the corners at an angle (Fig. C).

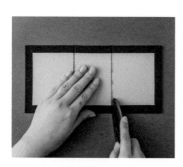

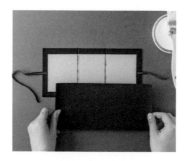

10. Apply starch glue to this bookbinding cloth, then wrap over paperboards ⓑ and ⓒ (Fig. C; page 19). With your paper folder, firmly press the folded cloth into the joint grooves. Then affix the ends of the ribbons into place with PVA glue.

11. Apply starch glue to the underside of the bookbinding cloth for the inner lining ⓓ, then fix into place, keeping the squares evenly spaced. Smooth firmly across the surface, then place weight on top and let rest overnight.

12. Apply PVA glue to the front and back of the pockets and affix to the case, evenly centered on the left and right and 15 mm from the top of the opening. Reach inside to smooth firmly.

#14

BOOKLET BOX

A set of linking boxes for small documents

These smaller-sized document boxes are perfect for keeping various items that tend to go stray, such as letters, postcards, and single-page documents. Due to their smaller size, each can be unstable when standing alone, but by adding slots on each side, the boxes can be chained together with V-shaped paper clips.

materials

- Box: 1 sheet 185 × 425 mm paper (approx. 350 gsm)
  (The example uses two kinds of paper glued together.)
- 12-mm (inside diameter) eyelet
- 4 V-shaped paper clips

size

figure

Figure (Box)

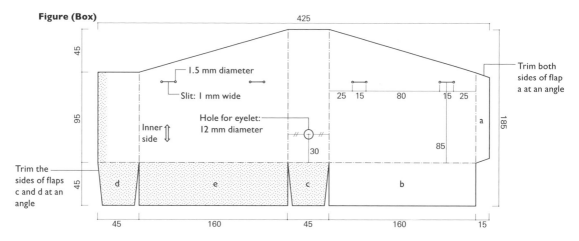

425

45

95

45

1.5 mm diameter

Slit: 1 mm wide

Hole for eyelet:
12 mm diameter

Inner ↑
side ↓

Trim both
sides of flap
a at an angle

25 15   80   15 25

a

185

85

30

Trim the
sides of flaps
c and d at an
angle

d   e   c   b

45   160   45   160   15

---

method

1. Score and crease the fold lines on the paper for the box (Fig.).

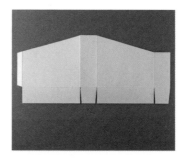

2. Cut the paper for the box into size and shape (Fig.).

3. Cut open the slits for the linking clips (Fig.; page 16).

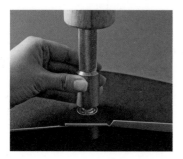

4. Set the eyelet for the front-side spine.

5. Apply the PVA glue for flap *a* and affix in place.

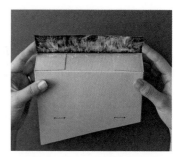

6. Glue together the flaps for the underside of the box starting with flap *b*, then *c* and *d*, and finally *e* as the outermost layer. While being careful not to crush the box, smooth to create a strong bond.

#14 BOOKLET BOX

RECEIPT ORGANIZER

A book of expanding folders for organizing a year of receipts

This organizer contains twelve pockets, each for storing one month of receipts. When opened flat, the pockets spread open like a peacock's feathers. Four elastic cords keep the organizer closed even as the pockets begin to fill and expand.

materials

- · Cover: 2 sheets 276 × 140 mm paper (approx. 115 gsm) ⓐ
- · Spine: 1 piece 276 × 60 mm bookbinding cloth ⓑ
- · Cover: 2 sheets 246 × 138 mm paperboard (2 mm thick) ⓒ
- · Inner lining: 2 sheets 240 × 132 mm paper
  (approx. 115 gsm) ⓓ
- · Spine lining: 1 sheet 240 × 60 mm paper (approx. 115 gsm) ⓔ
- · Pockets: 12 sheets 270 × 260 mm paper (approx. 115 gsm) ⓕ
- · 4 pieces approx. 290 mm elastic cord
- · 2 × 4-mm (inside diameter) eyelets

size

148

246

figures

Figure A (Pockets)

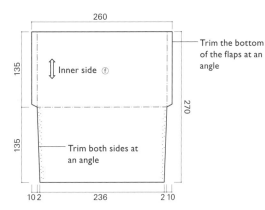

260
135
Inner side ⓕ
Trim the bottom of the flaps at an angle
270
135
Trim both sides at an angle
10 2   236   2 10

Figure B (Spine Cloth)

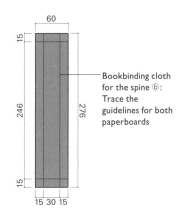

60
15
246   276
15
15 30 15

Bookbinding cloth for the spine ⓑ: Trace the guidelines for both paperboards

Figure C (Cover)

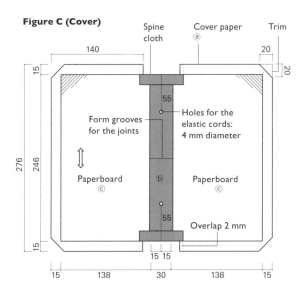

Spine cloth   Cover paper ⓐ   Trim
140   20
15   20
55
Form grooves for the joints
Holes for the elastic cords: 4 mm diameter
276   246
Paperboard ⓒ   ⓑ   Paperboard ⓒ
55
Overlap 2 mm
15
15 15
15   138   30   138   15

method

1. Score and crease the fold lines on the paper for the pockets ⓕ (Fig. A).

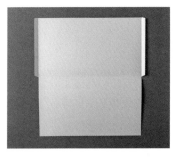

2. Trim the excess material from the paper for the pockets ⓕ (Fig. A).

3. Apply PVA glue to the glue areas and fold into the shape of a pouch. Make all 12 pockets, then place weight on top and let rest for a time.

4. Place a centered 50 × 80 mm strip of double-sided tape on the outside of the pockets, directly along the top edge. Tape the pockets together into a stack, taking care to keep their top openings aligned.

5. Trace the guidelines on the underside of the bookbinding cloth for the spine ⓑ (Fig. B).

6. Apply starch glue to the spine cloth and affix paperboards ⓒ, then wrap the cloth over the head and foot of the boards. Firmly press the joint grooves with a paper folder to create a solid bond.

(Overlap the spine cloth by 2 mm.)

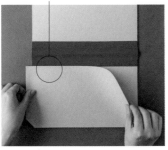

7. Apply starch glue onto the underside of the cover paper ⓐ, then affix to the outer side of the cover, while keeping the overhang evenly spaced across the head, foot, and fore edges (Fig. C).

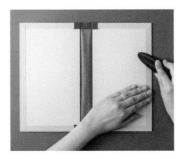

8. Turn the cover over and wrap the front and back cover paper around the head, foot, and fore edges (page 19).

9. Apply starch glue onto the underside of the spine lining paper ⓔ and affix to the inside of the spine, keeping the squares even. Use a paper folder to form a tight bond along the ridges.

10. Apply starch glue to the underside of the lining paper ⓓ and affix to the inside of the cover, keeping the squares even. Smooth firmly across the surface, then place weight on top and let rest overnight.

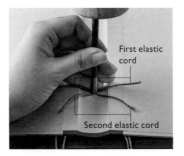

First elastic cord

Second elastic cord

11. Punch the holes in the spine and pass two elastic cords through each, so that a loop is formed on the outside of the cover, then affix with eyelets (page 21). Pay attention to the location and alignment of the cords as they pass through the holes.

(Keep the squares even along the head, foot, and fore edges.)

12. Place a 50 × 80 mm strip of double-sided tape to the front and back of the set of pouches, then affix to the cover. Reach inside the pocket to smooth firmly.

DOCUMENT ENVELOPE

A gusseted document folder

Document folders are typically made from kraft paper, but sometimes it's fun to try one with a different mood. I gave this envelope different colors inside and out, added a gusset made from bookbinding cloth, and upgraded the button and string. Why not try changing the shape and size of the upper flap? A folder like this can also be used in place of gift wrapping.

materials

- · Envelope: 1 sheet 190 × 685 mm paper (approx. 230 gsm)
  (The example uses two kinds of paper glued together.)
- · Gussets: 2 sheets 40 × 285 mm bookbinding cloth
- · Buttons: 2 × 15-mm diameter circles card stock
  (The example uses cloth fixed to card stock.)
- · 2 × 3.5-mm diameter double-cap rivets
- · 1 piece approx. 220 mm ribbon

size

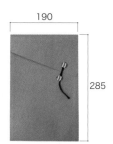

190

285

figures

Fig. A (Envelope)

Bookbinding cloth

Outer side
285

40

10

Crease at
5 mm intervals

685

40

c

20

Rounded
corners

a

Hole for the
button:
2 mm diameter

b

55

d

115

15 mm diameter

Cut a shallow angle toward
the center of the notch and
round with scissors.

Inner side

10

95

190

95

10

65 35 15

a

b

115

285

285

Hole for the button and
ribbon: 2 mm diameter

Fig. B (Button and Ribbon)

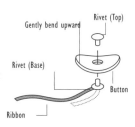

Gently bend upward

Rivet (Top)

Rivet (Base)

Button

Ribbon

Because the ribbon will need to
wrap around the buttons, select a
post length that will leave enough
room for your chosen ribbon.

method

1. Score and crease the fold lines on
the paper for the envelope (Fig. A).

2. Cut the upper flap at an angle
and round the corners with scissors.
Punch a hole into the throat to make
it easier to access your documents
(Fig. A). Then cut a shallow angle
toward the center of the notch and
round with scissors.

3. Score the bookbinding cloth, then
press with a paper folder to make
the creases.

4. Apply PVA glue to the 10-mm-
wide glue locations marked a, then
attach the folded bookbinding cloths
so that the proper sides face out.

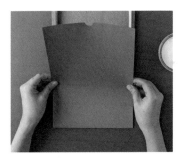

5. Apply PVA glue to the 10-mm-
wide glue locations marked b. While
holding the bookbinding cloths in
place, carefully fold the envelope into
its finished shape, working up from
the bottom fold. Set a weight on top
and let rest overnight.

6. Punch a hole in position c, then
insert the ribbon and fix the button
in place with a rivet (Fig. B; page
21). In position d, put only a button
and rivet.

DOCUMENT FOLDER

A document folder with pockets

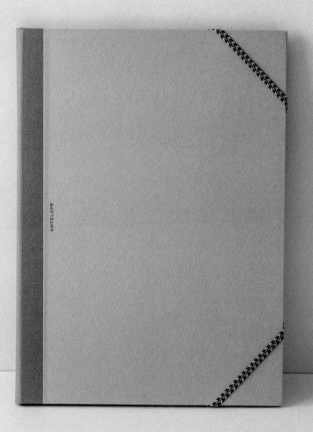

This A4-sized document folder has three additional smaller pockets to fit B5 paper, A5 paper, and business cards. I reinforced the pocket openings with folded-over paper or bookbinding cloth. Because larger-sized projects can be harder to work with, I recommend making some smaller items first.

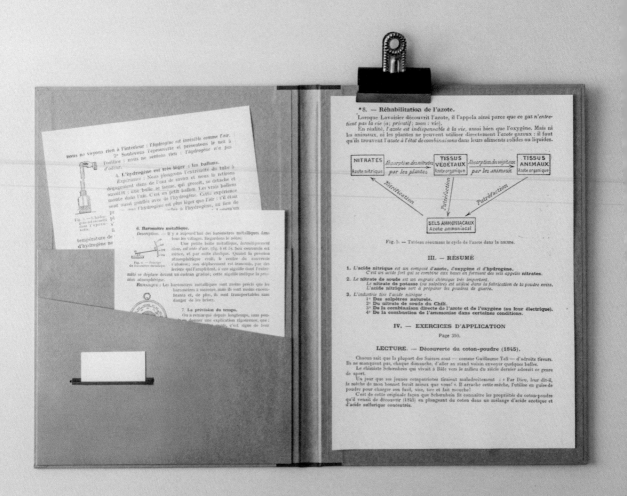

materials

· Cover: 2 sheets 350 × 227 mm paper (approx. 115 gsm) ⓐ
· Spine: 1 sheet 350 × 60 mm bookbinding cloth ⓑ
· Cover: 2 sheets 320 × 230 mm paperboard (2 mm thick) ⓒ
· Inner lining: 2 sheets 314 × 220 mm paper
   (approx. 115 gsm) ⓓ
· Spine lining: 1 sheet 314 × 50 mm paper (approx. 115 gsm) ⓔ
· Pockets (approx. 115 gsm) ⓕ:
   1 sheet 185 × 240 mm paper (medium);
   1 sheet 155 × 241 mm paper (small)
· Pockets: 2 pieces 8 × 70 mm bookbinding cloth ⓖ
· 2 pieces approx. 170 mm flat elastic cord
· 4 × 4-mm (inside diameter) eyelets

size

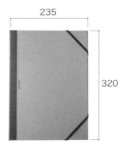

235

320

figures

Fig. A (Pockets)

Apply PVA glue and fold upon itself to reinforce the openings

[M]

5

180

185

Outer side ⓕ

Trim the corners of both side flaps at an angle

10 220 10

240

[S]

5

140

155

ⓕ

1.5 mm diameter
70

Slit: 4 mm wide

10

10 30 70 10

241

Fig. B (Spine Cloth)

Bookbinding cloth for the spine ⓑ: Trace the guidelines for both paperboards

60

15

15

320 350

15

15

20

Fig. C (Cover)

Cover paper ⓐ

Spine cloth

227

Trim

20 20

15

350 320

Form joint grooves

Paperboard ⓒ

20
90

Holes for the elastic cords: 4 mm diameter

90
20

ⓑ

Paperboard ⓒ

Overlap 2 mm

15

15 230 20 230 15

method

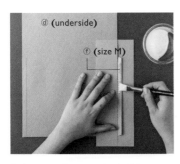

ⓓ (underside)

ⓕ (size M)

1. Score and crease the fold lines on the paper for the pockets ⓕ (Fig. A). Apply PVA glue to the flaps on the medium pocket and fix onto the lining paper ⓓ.

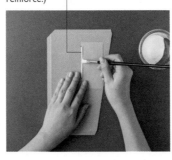

(Fold the bookbinding cloth in half and stick to the top and bottom openings to reinforce.)

2. Cut the slit into the small pocket (Fig. A; page 16) and glue the bookbinding cloth ⓖ to the lips of the opening. Apply PVA glue to the small pocket's flaps and fix onto the medium pocket.

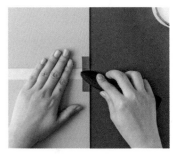

3. Trace guidelines onto the underside of the spine cloth ⓑ, then apply starch glue and affix the paperboards ⓒ. Fold the spine cloth over the head and foot (page 71, steps 5–6).

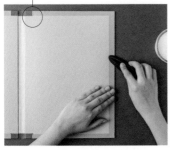

(Overlap the spine cloth by 2 mm.)

4. Apply starch glue to the underside of the cover paper ⓐ and wrap around the cover (Fig. C; page 71, steps 7–8).

5. Punch the holes in the cover, insert the elastic cords, and affix with eyelets (Fig. C; page 21). Be careful not to twist the elastic cords.

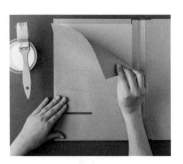

6. Paste the spine liner paper ⓔ, followed by the pockets on one side, and the remaining sheet of lining paper ⓓ on the other (page 71, steps 9–10). Do this quickly to avoid wrinkling from paper expansion.

MASKING TAPE BOX

A tape storage box with a pull-out drawer

Masking tape is one of those stationery supplies that I keep accumulating but struggle to store properly. I want it to be tidy and stored away, but I also want to be able to easily see which colors are where. This box is my solution, with round windows offering a view of the tape tucked away inside.

materials

- Drawer: 1 sheet 120 × 350 mm paper (approx. 350 gsm)
  (The example uses two kinds of paper glued together.)
- Outer case: 1 sheet 178 × 191 mm paper (approx. 350 gsm)
- Base: 1 sheet 117 × 187 mm paper (approx. 350 gsm)
- Pull: 40-mm long × 6-mm wide leather strap

(The example box holds 12 rolls of 15-mm wide, 35-mm diameter tape. When creating a box sized to store your own tape, make the box's internal dimensions 5–10 mm larger than the tape you wish to store.)

size

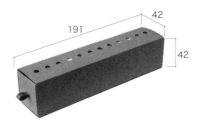

figures

Fig. A (Drawer)

Fig. B (Outer Case)

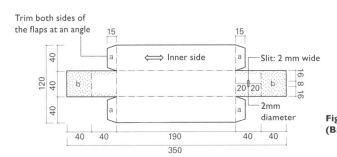

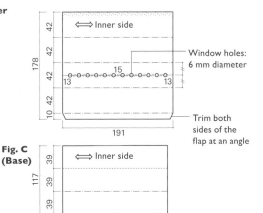

Fig. C (Base)

method

1. Score and crease the fold lines on the paper for the drawer (Fig. A).

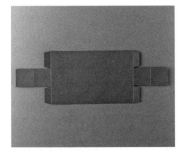

2. Cut the paper to size and shape (Fig. A).

3. Cut the slit for the leather pull (Fig. A; page 16). Bend the leather strap into a loop, insert the ends through the slit, and affix in place with PVA glue.

4. Apply PVA glue to the glue areas for the flaps labeled a and form the drawer. Apply double-sided tape to the flaps labeled *b* and fold inside.

5. Score and crease the paper for the outer case and punch open the window holes (Fig. B). Apply PVA glue to the glue area and form the case.

6. Score and crease the paper for the base (Fig. C) and insert into the drawer.

BOOK SLIPCASE

A slipcase for paperback books

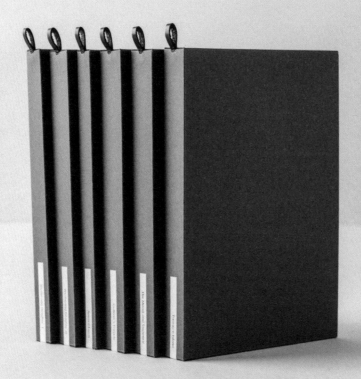

An array of matching slipcases looks absolutely beautiful on the shelf. This holds true even if the books themselves are paperbacks. I added a small leather pull at the top of the spine to make the cases and their books easy to retrieve. The small size and unobtrusive typeface of the labels suit the cases perfectly.

materials

· Case: 1 sheet paper (approx. 230 gsm)
· Book cover: 1 sheet glassine paper: (book's height + 60 mm) ×
  ([book's width × 2] + book's thickness + 100 mm)
· Pull: 40-mm long × 3-mm wide leather strap
· 1 label

(Note: Because books come in varying sizes and thicknesses, make each case
to fit your particular books.)

size

Book's width after
covering + 2 mm

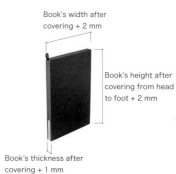

Book's height after
covering from head
to foot + 2 mm

Book's thickness after
covering + 1 mm

figures

Fig. A (Book Cover)

Place your book on the glassine paper and fold the paper around the book cover.

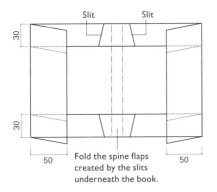

Slit   Slit

30

30

50   50

Fold the spine flaps created by the slits underneath the book.

Fig. B (Slipcase)

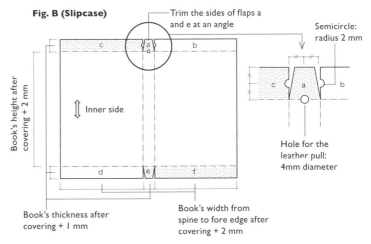

Trim the sides of flaps a and e at an angle

Semicircle: radius 2 mm

Book's height after covering + 2 mm

Inner side

c   a   b

d   e   f

c   a   b

Hole for the leather pull: 4mm diameter

Book's thickness after covering + 1 mm

Book's width from spine to fore edge after covering + 2 mm

method

1. If your book has a dust jacket, remove it. Wrap the book with glassine paper (Fig. A). For sizing the slipcase, measure the book with the glassine cover on. Measure the height (head to foot), width (spine to fore edge), and thickness.

2. Cut your paper for the slipcase to size and shape based on these measurements, then score and crease the folds (Fig. B).

3. Punch open the holes for the leather strap (one circular hole and two semicircles) (Fig. B).

4. Bend the leather strap into a loop and insert the ends through the hole. Apply PVA glue to flap *a* and fold over.

5. Form the head of the box and glue with PVA glue (being careful not to get glue on the leather strap). Fold flap *b* first and then flap *c*. Make sure all three holes for the strap are neatly aligned.

6. Form the foot of the box and glue with PVA glue, folding the flaps *d*, *e*, and *f* in that order. Insert your book and firmly smooth the head and foot sides. Affix a label of your choosing to the spine.

STORAGE BOX

Stackable storage boxes in three sizes

The large size holds 3.5" × 5" photographs, the medium size holds business cards, and the small size holds small objects such as sticky note flags and paper clips. The base of each size is double the surface area of the previous, which allows them to be stacked like building blocks. The rivets serve to reinforce the gluing and also make for a spiffy accent.

materials

· Box (approx. 230 gsm):
    1 sheet 306 × 346 mm paper (large);
    or 1 sheet 306 × 276 mm paper (medium);
    or 1 sheet 152 × 172 mm paper (small)
· Lid (approx. 230 gsm):
    1 sheet 300 × 340 mm paper (large);
    or 1 sheet 300 × 270 mm paper (medium);
    or 1 sheet 150 × 170 mm paper (small)
· 4 × 3.5-mm-diameter double-capped rivets

size

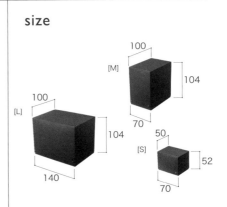

figures

Figure (Box and Lid)

Holes for the rivets (on lid only): 2 mm diameter

All dimensions are given in (box / lid) order.
The thickness of your paper or small variances in technique can make the boxes and lids too tight or too loose; adjust the measurements as necessary.

Trim the flap edges at an angle

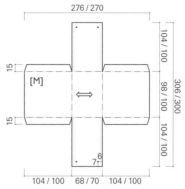

[L]

⟷ Inner side

346 / 340

104 / 100
98 / 100
104 / 100

306 / 300

15

15

104 / 100   138 / 140   104 / 100

6
7↑

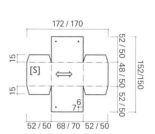

[M]

⟷

276 / 270

104 / 100
98 / 100
104 / 100

306 / 300

15

15

104 / 100   68 / 70   104 / 100

6
7↑

[S]

⟷

172 / 170

52 / 50
48 / 50
52 / 50

152/150

15

15

52 / 50   68 / 70   52 / 50

6
7↑

---

method

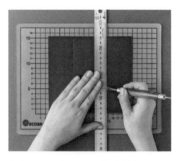

1. Score and crease the fold lines on the paper for the box (Fig.).

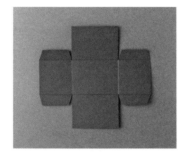

2. Cut the paper into size and shape (Fig.).

3. Form the box without gluing it. If any sides are higher than the others, trim the higher sides to fit. Make sure all four sides have matching heights.

4. Apply PVA glue to the glue areas and construct the box.

5. Firmly smooth the glued areas from the inside of the box. Construct the lid in the same method.

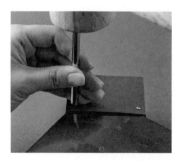

6. Set rivets into the lid. You can stack books or other objects to raise your riveting surface to a suitable height.

CONVERSION CHART

21 Photo Album

Cover	119 × 119mm	4.68 x 4.68in
Corner	70 x 70mm	2.75 x 2.75in
Paperboard	89 x 89mm	3.50 x 3.50in
Endpapers	83 x 83mm	3.26 x 3.26in
Photographs	89 x 89mm	3.50 x 3.50in

22 Collage Book

Cover wrapping	264 x 360mm	10.39 x 14.17in
Cover	180 x 276mm	7.08 x 10.87in
Text block	180 x 520mm	7.08 x 20.47in
Glassine paper	180 x 260mm	7.08 x 10.24in

23 Guest Book

Bookbinding cloth	131 x 473mm	5.16 x 18.62in
Cover	101 x 180mm	3.98 x 7.08in
Spine	101 x 24mm	3.98 x .94in
Endpapers	95 x 205mm	3.74 x 8.07in
Spine lining	95 x 35mm	3.74 x 1.38in
Text block	95 x 210mm	3.74 x 8.26in
Leather strap	300 x 5mm	11.81 x .20in

24 Photo Box

Box	595 × 660mm	23.42 × 25.98in
Lid	198 x 265mm	7.80 x 10.43in
Indexed pockets	131 x 2580mm	5.16 x 101.57in

25 Scrapbook

Cover	246 × 118mm	9.68 x 4.65 in
Spine	246 × 154mm	9.68 x 6.06in
Cover	216 × 154mm	8.50 x 6.06in
Spine	216 × 40mm	8.50 x 1.57in
Endpapers	210 × 148mm	8.26 x 5.82in
Spine lining	210 × 70mm	18.26 x 2.75in
Text block	210 × 297mm [A4]	8.26 x 11.69in

26 Ticket Binder

Cover	[envelope long side] + 50mm × [twice envelope short side] + 70mm	[envelope long side] + 1.97in × [twice envelope short side] + 2.75 in
Cover	[envelope long side] + 30mm × [twice envelope short side] + 50mm	[envelope long side] + 1.18in × [twice envelope short side] + 1.97 in

27 Accordion Book

Cover	45-100 x 45-100mm	1.77-3.94 x 1.77-3.94in
Paperboard	45-100 x 45-100mm	1.77-3.94 x 1.77-3.94in
Mounting	45–90 × 90–200mm	1.77-3.54 x 3.54-7.87in

28 Book for Seals

Cover	180 × 345mm	7.08 x 13.38in
Text block	180 × 230m-	7.08 x 9.05in

29 Collection Book

Tracing paper	182 × 260mm	7.16 x 10.24in
Mounting paper	91 × 55mm	3.58 x 2.16in
Mounting paper	280 × 5mm	11.02 x .20in

30 Portfolio

Cover panels	200 × 270mm	7.87 x 10.63in
Paperboard	182 × 249mm	7.16 x 9.80in
Text block	182 × 257mm [B5]	7.16 x 10.12in
Lightweight paper	182 × 257mm [B5]	7.16 x 10.12

4. ARCHIVING

#21

PHOTO ALBUM

A photo album and display

This simple photo album is bound by a single screw-in rivet at one corner. I made mine in a square shape. The photos are rotated on the rivet hinge for viewing. When standing with one photo out, the album acts as a display stand. The chosen photo is easily switched with another to fit your mood.

materials

· Cover: 2 sheets 119 × 119 mm paper (approx. 115 gsm)
· Corner: 1 piece 70 × 70 mm bookbinding cloth, cut diagonally into two equal triangles
· Cover: 2 sheets 89 × 89 mm paperboard (2 mm thick)
· Endpapers: 2 sheets 83 × 83 mm paper (wrapping or other decorative paper)
· Photographs (89 × 89 mm), totaling 25 mm thickness
· 30-mm long set screw post (also called a Chicago screw)

(Note: The example is an 89 × 89 mm square, but this project can be made to fit any size photographs by making the cover the same size as your photos.)

size

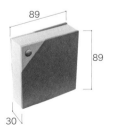

89

89

30

figures

Fig. A (Corner cloth)

70

20

20

70

Bookbinding cloth for the corner

Trim

Fig. B (Cover)

Corner cloth

15

89

15

65

15

15

89

65

119

Trim

Paperboard

Overlap 2 mm

20

15

20

119

Paper for the cover

Fig. C (Fastening)

Hole for the screw post: 4 mm diameter

Length of the screw post: Thickness of the two covers + thickness of all the photographs together

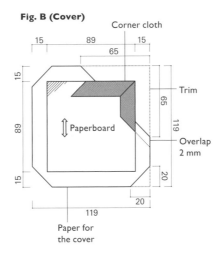

method

1. For the front and back covers: Trim the corner from your bookbinding cloth and attach to the paperboard with starch glue (Fig. A). (Mark 35 mm away from the corner on both sides, then connect to create your guideline.)

2. Wrap the bookbinding cloth around the paperboard (page 19).

(Overlap the corner cloth by 2 mm.)

3. Trim the corners of the cover paper (Fig. B). Apply starch glue to the underside of the cover paper and wrap around the paperboard (page 19).

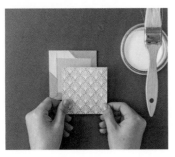

4. Apply starch glue to the underside of your endpaper and affix to the covers, keeping the squares evenly spaced. Smooth firmly, then place weight on top and let rest overnight.

(The position of the screw post corner is mirrored between the front and back covers.)

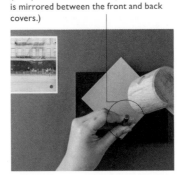

5. Punch the holes for the screw post in your photographs and the front and back covers (Fig. C). For the photographs, punch the hole (in the lower right corner) on one photo first, then use as a template for punching the others a few at a time.

6. Arrange the book in order (front cover, photos, back cover) and fasten with the screw post (Fig. C).

COLLAGE BOOK

A French-style collage book

Every page in this collage book is a gatefold page that opens outward beyond the boundary of the book. I added glassine paper between the pages to protect their contents, and the soft cover is wrapped in a French-style.

materials

- Cover wrapping: 1 sheet 264 × 360 mm paper
  (approx. 115 gsm) ⓐ
- Cover: 1 sheet 180 × 276 mm paper (approx. 230 gsm) ⓑ
- Text block: 4 sheets 180 × 520 mm paper
  (approx. 115 gsm) ⓒ
- 5 sheets 180 × 260 mm glassine paper ⓓ
- Hemp thread: 3 × height of text block from head to foot
- 1 label

size

140

184

figures

Fig. A (Text Block)

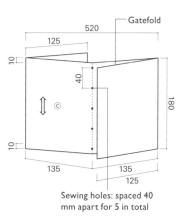

Gatefold

520
125
10
40
180
10
135   135
125
10

ⓒ

Sewing holes: spaced 40
mm apart for 5 in total

Fig. B (Page Arrangement)

When looking from above

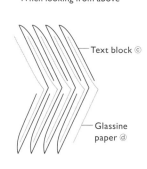

Text block ⓒ

Glassine
paper ⓓ

Fig. C (Cover Wrap)

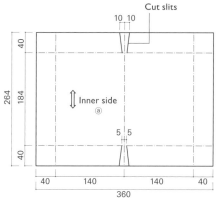

Cut slits

10 10

40
264
184
40

Inner side
ⓐ

5 5

40   140   140   40
360

method

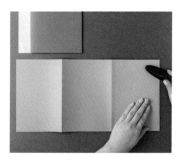

1. Fold the cover paper ⓑ and the glassine paper ⓓ in half with a paper folder. Fold the text block paper ⓒ so that both the front and reverse sides have a gatefold (Fig. A).

2. Layer the glassine paper ⓓ and the text block ⓒ so that the glassine paper lies inside each gatefold (Fig. B).

3. Place the cover paper ⓑ around the pages and punch the sewing holes (Fig. A), then sew with thread (page 26, steps 3–5).

4. Score and crease the fold lines on the paper for the cover wrap ⓐ and cut the slits (Fig. C). Apply PVA glue to the flaps between the slits and fold inside.

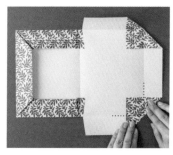

5. Fold the corners of the cover wrap and then the four sides.
(Fold the corners at an angle so that the side folds overlap straight.)

6. Tuck the cover of the book into the cover wrap, and glue the cover wrap together at the corners. Add a label of your choosing to the front.

GUEST BOOK

A guest book bound with a leather strap

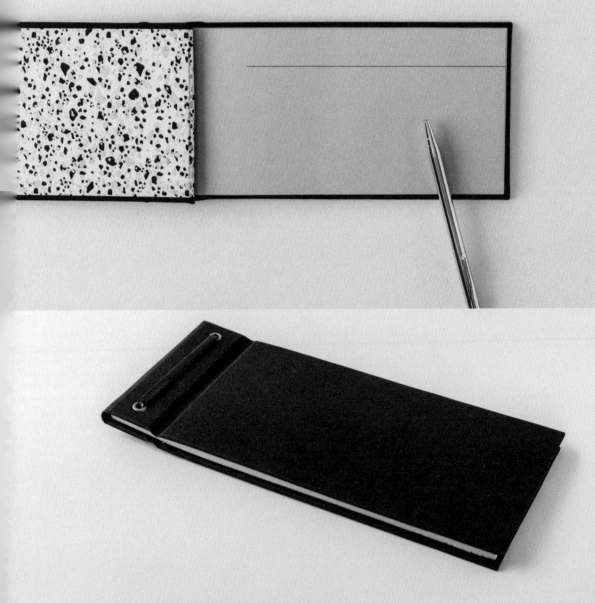

This highly versatile, compact guest book holds a separate page for each guest to sign. The body text can be easily removed by undoing the leather strap, which allows for the pages to be handed out to guests to be written upon at leisure, or for the page order and number of pages to be changed as needed.

materials

· Cover:
   131 × 473 mm bookbinding cloth ⓐ
   2 sheets 101 × 180 mm paperboard (2 mm thick) ⓑ
· Spine: 2 sheets 101 × 24 mm paperboard (2 mm thick) ⓒ
· Endpapers: 2 sheets 95 × 205 mm paper ⓓ
· Spine lining: 1 sheet 95 × 35 mm paper ⓔ
· Text block: several sheets 95 × 210 mm paper (enough for a
   total thickness of 3–6 mm) ⓕ
· 300-mm long × 5-mm wide leather strap
· 4 × 4-mm (inside diameter) eyelets

size

218

101

figures

Fig. A (Text Block)

Print ruled lines as desired.
Three pages can be made from one
sheet of A4 paper.

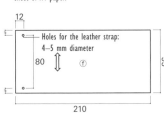

Holes for the leather strap:
4–5 mm diameter

12 · 80 · ⓕ · 95 · 210

Fig. B (Cover)

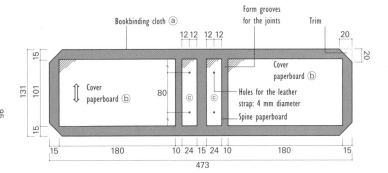

Bookbinding cloth ⓐ · Form grooves for the joints · Trim

12 12 12 12 · 20

Cover paperboard ⓑ · 15 · 131 · 101 · 80 · ⓒ · ⓒ · 20

Cover paperboard ⓑ

Holes for the leather strap: 4 mm diameter

Spine paperboard

15 · 15 · 180 · 10 24 15 24 10 · 180 · 15 · 473

---

method

1. Use an 80 mm center-to-center
two-hole punch (or a hollow punch)
to open the holes for the leather
strap in the paper for the text block
ⓕ (Fig. A).

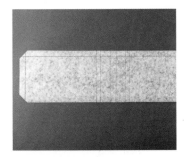

2. On the underside of the
bookbinding cloth ⓐ, trace guidelines
15 mm from the head and left sides
as well as the guidelines for the joint
grooves, then trim the corners (Fig. B).

3. Apply starch glue to the
bookbinding cloth ⓐ and wrap
around paperboards ⓑ and ⓒ (Fig. B;
page 19). Use a paper folder to form
a tight bond along the ridges.

4. Keeping the squares evenly
spaced, fix the spine lining ⓔ, then
the endpapers ⓓ (page 71, step 9) to
the cover. Smooth firmly, then place
weight on top and let rest overnight.

5. Punch open the holes for the leather
strap (Fig. B) and set the eyelets.

6. Arrange the text block from
step 1 inside the cover. Pass the
leather strap through and tie on the
underside of the book.

PHOTO BOX

An indexed box for archiving photographs

I always want to print out my photographs but don't have the time to make photo albums for all of them—separating the photos by month and archiving them in a box is more feasible. I put twelve indexed pockets into the box and add a new box each year.

materials

· Box: 1 sheet 595 × 660 mm paper (approx. 350 gsm)
· Lid: 1 sheet 198 × 265 mm paper (approx. 350 gsm)
· Indexed pockets: 1 sheet 131 × 2580 mm paper
  (approx. 350 gsm; smaller sheets can be glued together)
· 12 labels

size

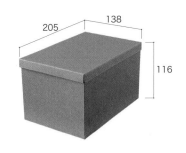

figures

Fig. A (Box)

If flaps b and c are fitting too tightly when folded over, trim about 1 mm from the sides of the flaps.

Trim the sides of the flaps at an angle

⟵⟶ Inner side

15   15

115

115

115

135

595

115

115

115   115   200   115   115

660

a   a

b   b

a   a

c

c

Fig. B (Lid)

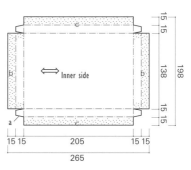

⟵⟶ Inner side

15 15
138
198
15 15

15 15   205   15 15

265

c

b   b

a

c

Fig. C (Index)

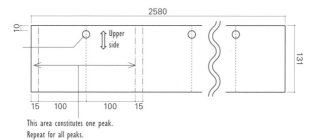

Holes for the labels: 15 mm diameter

2580

10

⇅ Upper side

131

15   100   100   15

This area constitutes one peak. Repeat for all peaks.

Side view of the index

100

15   15

---

method

1. Score and crease the fold lines for the box (Fig. A).

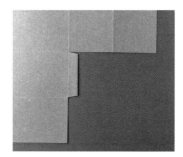

2. Cut the paper to size and shape (Fig. A).

3. Apply PVA glue to the glue areas for flaps and to construct the box shape.

4. Apply double-sided tape to flaps b and c and fold into the box.

5. Reach inside the box to firmly smooth all the glued sides.

6. Construct the lid in the same manner (Fig. B) and firmly smooth the glued sides.

7. Score and crease the paper for the indexed pockets (Fig. C).

8. If your paper is not long enough, join multiple sheets of paper with a strip of starch glue, ensuring there is a 15 mm overlap. Continue until you have made twelve peaks.

9. Punch holes for the labels at the top of the peaks (Fig. C).

(Fold the label in half and make readable from both sides.)

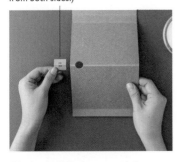

10. Apply PVA glue around the underside of the label holes and affix each label from below, with the labels visible through the holes.

11. Stick the front and back of each mountain peak together with double-sided tape.

12. Using double-sided tape, stick the frontmost 15 mm base of the index to the base of the box.

SCRAPBOOK

A scrapbook with three-hole binding

This hardbound scrapbook contains a plentiful 320 pages. The binding uses the simplest of the bookbinding stitches repeated in parallel. The spine—an area of frequent damage and wear—is reinforced with cloth, and the corners are given metal corner protectors. The lay-flat pages make this scrapbook easy to work with and view.

materials

- · Cover: 2 sheets 246 × 118 mm paper (approx. 115 gsm) ⓐ
- · Spine: 1 piece 246 × 154 mm bookbinding cloth ⓑ
- · Cover: 2 sheets 216 × 154 mm paperboard (2 mm thick) ⓒ
- · Spine: 1 sheet 216 × 40 mm paperboard (2 mm thick) ⓓ
- · Endpapers: 2 sheets 210 × 148 mm paper (approx. 115 gsm) ⓔ
- · Spine lining: 1 sheet 210 × 70 mm paper (approx. 115 gsm) ⓕ
- · Text block: 80 sheets 210 × 297 mm (A4) paper (kraft paper, etc.) ⓖ
- · Hemp thread: 3 × height of text block from head to foot (per signature)
- · 12 × 4-mm (inside diameter) eyelets
- · 4 × 2.5-mm (inside diameter) metal book corner protectors

size

156

216

43

figures

Fig. A (Text Block)

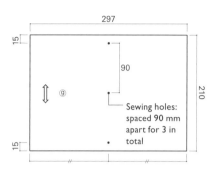

297

15

90

210

ⓖ

Sewing holes:
spaced 90 mm
apart for 3 in
total

15

Fig. B (Spine Cloth)

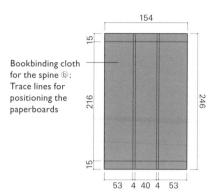

154

15

Bookbinding cloth
for the spine ⓑ:
Trace lines for
positioning the
paperboards

216

246

15

53 4 40 4 53

Fig. C (Cover)

Spine cloth ⓑ

Overlap
2 mm

Trim

118

4   4

20

15

20

Form grooves
for the joints

ⓓ

216

246

Cover
paperboard ⓒ

Cover
paperboard ⓒ

Cover
paper ⓐ

Spine paperboard

15

15   154   40   154   15

Fig. D (Spine)

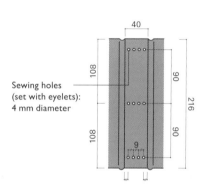

40

108

90

Sewing holes
(set with eyelets):
4 mm diameter

216

108

90

9

method

1. Fold the text block paper ⓖ in half with a paper folder (page 17) and place in stacks of ten. Each stack will constitute one signature. Make eight signatures (page 50, step 2).

2. Mark the locations of the sewing holes on the inside fold of the innermost page of each signature (Fig. A).

3. Open the first signature at a 90-degree angle, then punch open the sewing holes at a 45-degree angle using an awl. Repeat for the remaining signatures.

4. Trace the guidelines on the underside of the bookbinding cloth for the spine ⓑ (Fig. B).

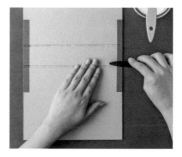

5. Apply starch glue to the cloth, affix paperboards ⓒ and ⓓ, and wrap the head and foot of the cloth around them. Use a paper folder to form a tight bond along the ridges.

(Overlap the spine cloth by 2 mm.)

6. Apply starch glue to the underside of the cover paper ⓐ and wrap around the paperboards (Fig. C; page 71, steps 7–8).

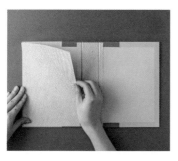

7. Attach the spine lining ⓕ (page 71, step 9) and endpapers ⓔ to the cover, keeping the squares evenly spaced. Smooth firmly, then place weight on top and let rest overnight.

8. Punch the sewing holes through the spine and set eyelets in each hole (Fig. D).

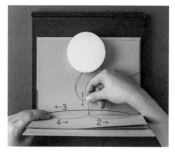

9. Sew the first signature of the text block onto the cover (page 20): Begin sewing the first signature through the lowermost set of sewing holes.

10. End the signature's stitch with a square knot on the inside of the text block and trim the excess thread. Repeat with the second signature, also using the lowermost set of sewing holes.

(Correct any twisting or tangling of the thread as you stitch.)

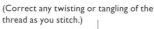

11. For the third signature, stitch through the set of sewing holes second from the bottom. Proceed sewing the remaining signatures, sewing two signatures into each set of holes.

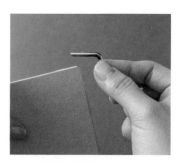

12. Slightly trim the corners of the covers to fit your corner protectors, then apply a small amount of PVA glue to both the corners and the protectors and affix.

#26

TICKET BINDER

A ticket binder made with envelopes

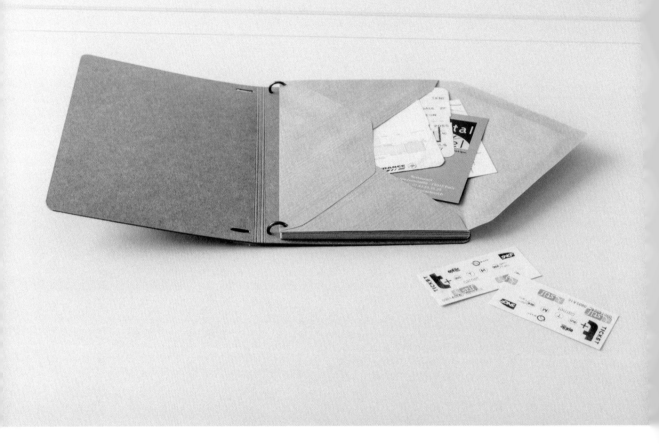

This is a casual-style binder made from commercially available envelopes held in place with jump rings. Let this be a home for paper mementos—tickets from travels, movie and museum stubs, business cards, and so on. You could also use semi-transparent envelopes so that the contents can be seen at a glance.

materials

· Cover:
   1 piece bookbinding cloth (envelope long side +
   50 mm) × (twice envelope short side + 70 mm)
   1 sheet paper (approx. 350 gsm): (envelope long side + 30 mm)
   × (twice envelope short side + 50 mm),
· 8–12 envelopes (enough for a total thickness of 3–4 mm)
· Elastic cord: 2 × height of the cover from head to foot
· 2 × 2-mm-thick, 10-mm (inside diameter) jump rings
· 4-mm (inside diameter) eyelet

size

envelope short side
+14mm

envelope long
side +6mm

figures

Fig. A (Envelopes)

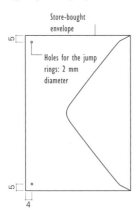

Store-bought envelope

Holes for the jump rings: 2 mm diameter

5
5
4

Fig. B (Cover)

Holes for the jump rings: 2 mm diameter

10 3 3 10

Rounded corners

8

8

Slits: 2 mm wide

Inner side

Score and crease at 2 mm intervals

Hole for the elastic cord: 4 mm diameter

Envelope long side + 6 mm

Envelope short side + 12 mm

6

Envelope short side + 12 mm

method

1. Punch the holes for the jump rings through one envelope (Fig. A), then use as a template for punching the others a few at a time.

2. Apply starch glue to the underside of the cover paper and affix to the underside of the bookbinding cloth. Smooth firmly, then place weight on top and let rest overnight.

3. Trim the cover to size and shape. Score and crease the spine and round the corners with a corner punch (Fig. B).

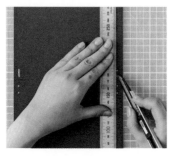

4. Open the holes for the jump ring. Punch holes in the back cover and cut a slit the thickness of the jump ring on the front cover (Fig. B; page 16).

5. Punch a hole for the elastic cord in the back cover, then pass the ends of the cord through and fasten in place with an eyelet (page 21).

6. Insert the jump rings into the holes from step 4, then insert the envelopes and close the rings (page 21).

ACCORDION BOOK

A house-shaped accordion fold book

This is an accordion-folded book that you'll want to keep making in different shapes—like the steeple of a church or the sawtooth roof of a factory. The small book can function as a stamp book or an album for mini photographs. It can also stand like a folding screen to be enjoyed as if you were browsing the shelves of a curio shop.

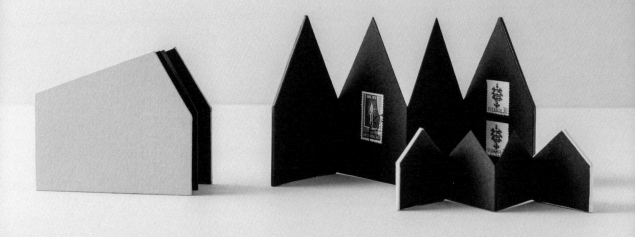

materials

· Cover:
    2 sheets paper (approx. 115 gsm)
    2 sheets paperboard (2 mm thick)
· Mounting: 3 sheets 45–100 × 90–200 mm paper
        (approx. 230 gsm)

(Note: The above range is the suggested size; make any size you please.)

size

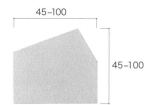

45–100

45–100

figures

Fig. A (Text Block)

The mounting paper, as viewed from above

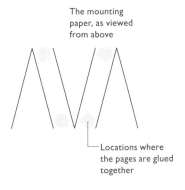

Locations where the pages are glued together

Fig. B (Cover)

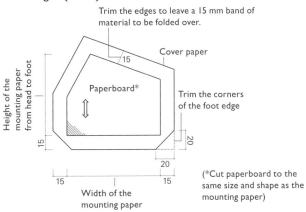

Trim the edges to leave a 15 mm band of material to be folded over.

Cover paper

15

Paperboard*

Trim the corners of the foot edge

20

20

Height of the mounting paper from head to foot

15

15

15

Width of the mounting paper

(*Cut paperboard to the same size and shape as the mounting paper)

method

1. Score and fold the mounting paper in half, then arrange with the folded edges on alternating sides.

2. Lay the stack of mounting pages flat, then spread 3-mm-wide strips of PVA glue between the pages to stick both sides together (Fig. A).

3. Cut the head edge of the mounting pages into a triangle shape. Apply a small amount of PVA glue into the peaks of the pockets of the double-layered pages to hold them together.

4. Cut the paper for the front cover (15 mm larger than the mounting pages on all sides). On the underside, trace guidelines 15 mm from the foot and left edges, and trim the corners of the foot edge.

(Use a paper folder to fold the edges of the triangle shape.)

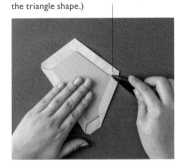

5. Cut the paperboard into the same shape as the mounting pages. Apply starch glue to the underside of the cover paper and wrap over the paperboard (Fig. B; page 19). Repeat with the back cover (whose shape will mirror the front).

6. Apply PVA glue to the outside of the first and last mounting pages and glue to the covers. Smooth firmly, then place weight on top and let rest overnight.

BOOK FOR SEALS

A goshuincho made with wet-torn washi

A *goshuincho* is a book for receiving official shrine and temple seals to commemorate pilgrimages. The custom has seen a recent swell of popularity among Japanese people and tourists. This handmade book makes full use of the texture and character of washi. The edges are deckled by wet tearing, and the cover uses the same paper for an elegant but natural appearance. Because the book is quite fragile, I made an accompanying case.

materials

- · Cover: 2 sheets 180 × 345 mm washi
- · Text Block: several sheets 180 × 230 mm washi (enough for a
  total thickness of 10–15 mm when folded in half and stacked)
  (Wet tear the head and foot edges of the washi [page 16] and cut the left and
  right edges cleanly with a craft knife.)
- · Case: 1 sheet paper (approx. 230 gsm)
  (The example uses two kinds of paper glued together.)

size

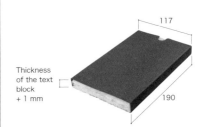

117

Thickness
of the text
block
+ 1 mm

190

figures

Fig. A (Text Block)

As viewed from above

Locations for glue

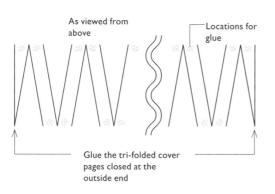

Glue the tri-folded cover pages closed at the outside end

Fig. B (Case)

15 mm diameter

Round the corner with scissors

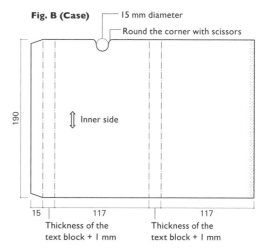

190

Inner side

15

117

Thickness of the text block + 1 mm

117

Thickness of the text block + 1 mm

method

(Washi for the cover)

1. Fold the text block pages in half with a paper folder, and the cover pages into thirds, accordion style. Arrange the pages with the folded edges on alternating sides (Fig. A).

2. Lay the stack of pages flat, then spread 3-mm-wide strips of starch paste between the pages to paste both sides together (Fig. A).

3. Glue the tri-folded front and back cover pages closed at their outside ends (Fig. A). Place weight on top and let rest overnight.

4. Measure the thickness of the book, then cut the paper for the case to size. Score and crease the fold lines on the case paper (Fig. B).

5. Cut a notch at the head of the case to make the book easier to pull out (Fig. B).

6. Spread PVA glue on the glue area and construct the case. Insert the book inside and firmly smooth the glued areas.

COLLECTION BOOK

A book made from tracing paper for storing flower specimens

I assembled my collection of pressed flowers into a single book. The text block and cover are made from tracing paper, which lends a delicate appearance. The binding is reinforced with leather straps, and the contents of the gatefold pages can be easily switched out.

materials

- Cover and text block: 21 sheets 182 × 260 mm tracing paper
- Mounting: 20 sheets 91 × 55 mm paper (business card size)
  (The example uses washi business cards.)
- Hemp thread: 3 × height of text block from head to foot
- 2 × approx. 280-mm long × 5-mm wide leather straps

  (In addition to the above materials, paperboard is needed during the sewing step.)

size

130

182

figures

Fig. A (Front Cover, Text Block) Adjust the locations of the slits so that your mounting paper will be centered on the page

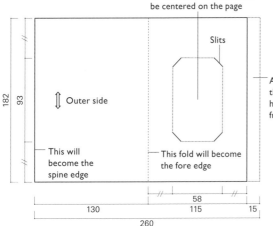

Slits

Outer side

This will become the spine edge

This fold will become the fore edge

After folding the paper in half, trim off from this side

182
93
130 | 58 | 115 | 15
260

Fig. B (Spine Edge of Front Cover)

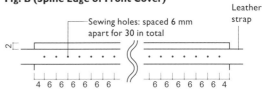

Leather strap

Sewing holes: spaced 6 mm apart for 30 in total

2

4 6 6 6 6 6 6   6 6 6 6 6 6 4

Fig. C (Arranging the Pages)

When viewed from above

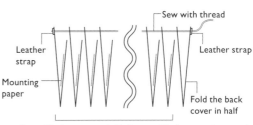

Sew with thread

Leather strap

Leather strap

Mounting paper

Fold the back cover in half

The front cover and text block pages are folded over with the mounting area inside. (Open the pages before sewing and fold them back again when you're done.)

Fig. D (Stitching)

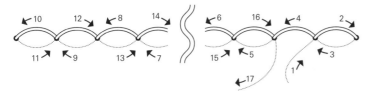

10   12   8   14   6   16   4   2

11   9   13   7   15   5   3

1

17

Enter through the second hole from the end. Fasten the beginning and end of the stitch near the sewing hole with a square knot. Follow this same stitching pattern even if you use a different amount of sewing holes in your book.

---

method

1. Glue the objects you wish to display (such as pressed flowers) onto the mounting paper.

2. Fold each piece of tracing paper in half with a paper folder (page 17).

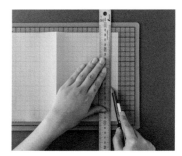

3. Open 20 of the folded pieces of tracing paper and trim 15 mm from their right side (Fig. A). Leave the last piece of tracing paper uncut for use as the back cover.

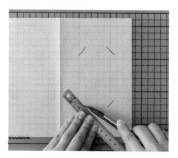

4. Cut slits into the 20 trimmed pieces of tracing paper to hold the mounting paper. Cut one page first, then use as a template for the others (Fig. A).

(Attach the strap to the end of the longer, uncut side of the folded page.)

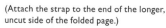

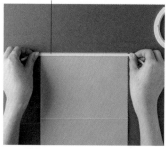

5. Using double-sided tape, fix the leather straps 2mm away from the edge of one of the trimmed pages (this will be the front cover) and the untrimmed back cover page.

6. Mark the locations for the sewing holes on the leather strap of the front cover (Fig. B).

(Let the leather straps extend from the paperboards.)

7. Assemble the book in order (Fig. C; unfolded front cover, text block, folded back cover) and hold in place with hinge clips (use paperboard to protect your tracing paper) and masking tape.

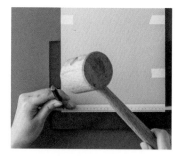

8. Punch open the sewing holes, straight up-and-down with your awl and not at an angle. As you work, keep verifying that everything is still in place as tracing paper can easily slip.

9. Sew the spine (Fig. D; page 20).

10. Secure the stitch with a square knot, then trim the excess thread. Apply a small amount of PVA glue to the tip of your awl and use it to push the knot into the sewing hole.

11. Remove the paperboards, insert your mounts from step 1 into their pages, and close the cover and text block pages (Fig. C).

12. Due to the book's fragile nature, store in a box or other container (see pages 84–85 for instructions on making a box).

PORTFOLIO

A minimalist portfolio

A created this simple portfolio to store my own artwork and photographs, just like that of a professional artist or photographer. The minimalistic style pairs well with any work of art.

materials

- · Cover panels:
   2 sheets 200 × 270 mm paper (approx. 115 gsm) ⓐ
   2 sheets 182 × 249 mm paperboard (2 mm thick) ⓑ
- · Text block cover: 1 sheet paper (approx. 230 gsm) ⓒ
- · Text block: 15–20 sheets 182 × 257 mm (B5) paper (approx. 150 gsm; enough for a total thickness of 4–6 mm) ⓓ
- · 2 sheets 182 × 257 mm (B5) lightweight paper (approx. 35 gsm) ⓔ
- · 1 strip cheesecloth ⓕ
- · Spine lining: 1 sheet paper (kraft paper) ⓖ
- · 1 label

(In addition to the above materials, kraft paper and paperboard are needed when gluing the spine.)

size

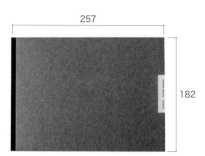

257

182

figures

Fig. A (Cheesecloth, Spine Lining)

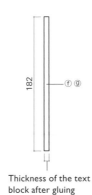

182

ⓕ ⓖ

Thickness of the text
block after gluing

Fig. B (Cover Paper)

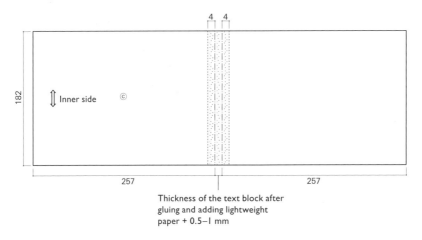

4 4

182

Inner side ⓒ

257   257

Thickness of the text block after
gluing and adding lightweight
paper + 0.5–1 mm

---

method

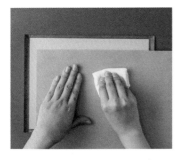

1. Make two exterior cover panels,
front and back: Apply starch glue to the
underside of the paper for the cover
panels ⓐ and stick to the paperboards
ⓑ. Smooth firmly, then place weight
on top and let rest overnight.

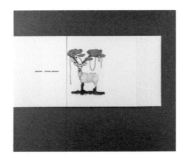

2. Print your works on the text block
paper ⓓ and arrange the pages in order.
Because the binding edge will disappear
into the binding, leave a small safety
margin (gutter) when printing.

(Ensure the spine edge extends beyond
the paperboard.)

3. Place the text block between two
pieces of kraft paper the same size as
the block. Then place between two
pieces of paperboard approximately
30 mm narrower, aligning the edge of
the pages. Hold in place with masking
tape and hinge clips.

4. Place the stack of paper between books or other heavy objects and apply PVA glue to the spine using your finger. Be careful not to get glue on the head or foot sides of the text block.

5. Gently turn up the spine and work the PVA glue between the pages, being careful not to fold the text block pages.

6. Gently bend the spine the other direction and work the PVA glue between the pages as before.

7. Return the spine to the level position, then apply PVA glue down the spine one more time. When finished, pinch along the spine to remove any swelling.

8. Measure the spine, then cut the cheesecloth and spine lining to size (Fig. A). Glue the cheesecloth ⓕ to the spine, then apply more PVA glue on top of the cheesecloth. Attach the spine lining ⓖ and smooth firmly.

9. Remove the paperboard and kraft paper from the text block. Apply a 3-mm-wide band of PVA glue to the spine edge of the first page of the text block and attach lightweight paper ⓔ. Repeat with the last page of the text block.

(Align with the head and fore edge of the book.)

10. Measure the thickness of the text block, then cut the text block cover paper ⓒ to size. Score and crease (Fig. B).

11. Apply PVA glue to the glue area on the text block cover paper and the spine of the text block. With the cover folded into a U-shape, push the spine into the cover and fix in place, applying pressure to keep the spine flat.

12. Trim the excess paper on the cover panels from step 1 to the size of their paperboards ⓑ. Apply starch glue to the underside of the front panel and fix to the front of the book. Repeat with the back panel on the back of the book. Smooth firmly, then place weight on top and let rest overnight.

#20 STORAGE BOX

AFTERWORD

I began making stationery because of a bookbinding class I took in England many years ago. Folding paper with a bone folder, sewing with thread, binding with glue—every step of the process was a delight. The classroom couldn't contain me; I was spreading my tools across my apartment dining table and working industriously at the craft.

My elder classmates, who had been practicing for many, many years, were pursuing styles of bookbinding with a long, artistic tradition, such as recasing antique and rare books in fine leather covers. I wasn't so interested in creating works of art; rather, I was completely focused on making a new notebook, which I could use at class the next day and would be a little bit special. I could use bookbinding skills to create stationery—practical, daily use items—with extra functions to assist with writing, organizing, and archiving.

After I returned to Japan, I got an opportunity to work in product development and planning for a stationery company. Japanese stationery is top-notch. I was forced to focus intently on design, coming up with ideas one after another, and sometimes combining two or three functions just to try to fill in the tiny gaps of unanswered consumer demand. But every time I developed a new product, somewhere inside I would think, truly good stationery should be much simpler.

I began to want to make my own stationery by hand, just like when I was in London and captivated by bookbinding. These would not be mass-produced goods but stationery that was unique and only for me. Working on the weekends, I made my own collection; and they became this book.

I've come to believe that truly good stationery are the ones you can use with fondness. And fondness is cultivated when you single out the things you like and use them for a long time—and of course when you make them with your own hands. If you pour your heart into making your own unique stationery, they may become a part of you and even give you goosebumps when you take them in hand. This is worth something far more than ease of use and convenience.

For the past several years, I've been relearning bookbinding as an art, this time in Japan. I wanted to understand the roots of the practical side of bookbinding which has so strongly captivated me. Twenty years later, I'm now following in the footsteps of my classmates. To study the techniques of bygone times— through sparing no effort, taking time, and making by hand—is to continuously examine the meaning of working with one's hands. I can feel this influence not just in my bookbinding or my work as an editor, but in my daily life. The true joy of making may not lie in the finishing of any one item, or in its use; but in the widening and deepening of thought that comes from the moving of one's hands.

Aya Nagaoka

Photo by masaco

INDEX

NORTH AMERICA

Published in the United States by Hardie Grant North America, an imprint of Hardie Grant Publishing Pty Ltd.

Hardie Grant North America
2912 Telegraph Ave
Berkeley, CA 94705
hardiegrantusa.com

© First Edition 2021 Elwin Street Ltd
Elwin Street Productions
10 Elwin Street
London E2 7BU, UK
elwinstreet.com

Original title: SHUMATSU DE TSUKURU KAMI BUNGU by Aya Nagaoka
© 2017 Aya Nagaoka © 2017 Graphic-sha Publishing Co., Ltd.
First designed and published in Japan in 2017 by Graphic-sha Publishing Co, Ltd. English translation rights arranged with
Graphic-sha Publishing Co, Ltd., through Japan UNI Agency, Inc., Tokyo.

Design: Fumiyo Moriya
Photography: Nao Shimizu, except page 125: masaco
Illustration: Kobushi Nakata
Text: Aya Nagaoka
Project Management: Yuko Miyago
English translation: Nathan Collins

Library of Congress Cataloging-in-Publication Data is available upon request.

Japanese Paper Craft
ISBN 9781958417652

10 9 8 7 6 5 4 3 2 1

Printed in China